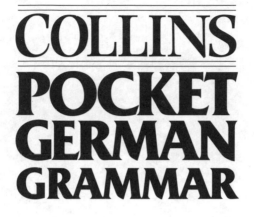

COLLINS
POCKET
GERMAN
GRAMMAR

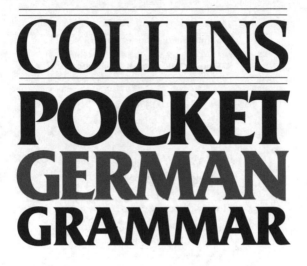

COLLINS
POCKET
GERMAN
GRAMMAR

HarperCollins*Publishers*

First published in this edition 1994

© **HarperCollins Publishers 1994**

ISBN 0 00 470156-9

Ilse MacLean
Lorna Sinclair-Knight

editorial staff
Horst Kopleck, Megan Thomson

editorial management
Vivian Marr

*A catalogue record for this book
is available from the British Library*

*Typeset by Morton Word Processing Ltd,
Scarborough*

*Printed in Great Britain by
HarperCollins Manufacturing, Glasgow*

INTRODUCTION

Your **Collins Pocket German Grammar** has been designed to give you maximum help in getting to grips with the basic features of the German language. If your knowledge of German grammar is elementary, non-existent or just rusty, this book provides all the essential information you need in a clear, easy-to-understand layout. For those who are already familiar with the structure of German, it provides an invaluable tool for reference and revision.

The book is divided into sections according to part of speech (noun, adjective, adverb etc) or grammar point (sentence structure, numbers, punctuation etc). Wherever we have used what may be unfamiliar technical terms, we have tried to give a brief explanation (or illustration) at the relevant point in the text.

One of the most innovative features of this book is the use of colour to highlight the learning points in each section. You can see at a glance exactly which grammar point is being illustrated to make learning easy – and fast!

Another important feature is the clear demarcation of grammatical points, illustrated by numerous examples. For instance, if you turn to page 60, you will see a series of bracketed numbers, (→**1**) to (→**11**), in colour throughout the page. These numbers cross-refer you to an example, or group of examples, correspondingly numbered in colour, on page 61. This double-page layout gives you maximum accessibility to the grammar point you are trying to learn or revise. And the practical, up-to-date examples help to fix that grammar point firmly in your mind.

The examples which illustrate each grammar point put special emphasis on contemporary German, without ignoring the more literary aspects of the language. Attention has also been paid to areas in which German usage differs from English usage, as in the sections on articles and prepositions. And in the section on sentence structure, we have tried to show you how to deal with word order problems, one of the most common pitfalls for the learner.

The fully comprehensive index at the end of the book lists subject references as well as key words in both German and English.

ABBREVIATIONS USED

acc	accusative	**ff**	and following pages	**nom**	nominative
contd	continued	**gen**	genitive	**pl**	plural
dat	dative	**masc**	masculine	**p(p)**	page(s)
fem	feminine	**neut**	neuter	**sing**	singular

4   CONTENTS

		Page
VERBS	Simple tenses	6
	The imperative	18
	Compound tenses	22
	Reflexive verbs	30
	The passive	34
	Impersonal verbs	42
	The infinitive	46
	Participles	50
	Modal verbs	52
	Use of tenses	58
	Uses of the subjunctive	62
	Verbs with prefixes	68
	Verbs taking prepositions	76
	Verbs taking the dative	80
	"There is/There are"	82
	Impersonal "es"	84
	List of strong and mixed verbs	86
NOUNS	Declension	98
	Gender	100
	The cases	108
	Forming plurals	112
	Proper nouns	116
	Measurement and quantity	116
ARTICLES	The definite article	118
	The indefinite article	124
	Words declined like the definite article	128
	Words declined like the indefinite article	136
	Indefinite adjectives	138
ADJECTIVES	Declension	140
	Participles as adjectives	146
	Adjectives taking the dative	146
	Adjectives used as nouns	148

		Page
	Adjectives of nationality etc	150
	Comparative and superlative	152
PRONOUNS	Personal pronouns	158
	Possessive pronouns	166
	Reflexive pronouns	170
	Relative pronouns	174
	Interrogative pronouns	178
	Indefinite pronouns	182
ADVERBS	Use of adverbs	188
	Formation of adverbs	190
	Adverbs of place	192
	Comparative and superlative	194
	"Emphasizers"	196
PREPOSITIONS	Taking the dative	202
	Taking the accusative	206
	Taking either dative or accusative	210
	Taking the genitive	212
CONJUNCTIONS	Co-ordinating conjunctions	214
	Subordinating conjunctions	220
SENTENCE STRUCTURE	Word order	224
	Separable verbs	230
	Question forms	232
	Negatives	234
NUMBERS	Cardinal and ordinal numbers	236
	Fractions and decimals	237
	The time	238
	The calendar	239
PUNCTUATION		240
INDEX		242

Tense Formation

Tenses are either **simple** or **compound**. Once you know how to form the past participle, compound tenses are similar for all verbs (see pp 22 to 29). To form simple tenses you need to know whether a verb is **weak, strong** or **mixed**.

Simple Tenses

In German these are:

Present indicative   (→**1**)
Imperfect indicative   (→**2**)
Present subjunctive   (→**3**)
Imperfect subjunctive   (→**4**)

Subjunctive forms are widely used in German, especially for indirect or reported speech (see pp 66 and 67).

The simple tenses are formed by adding endings to a verb **stem**. The endings show the number, person and tense of the subject of the verb (→**5**)

The types of verb you need to know to form simple tenses are:
● **Strong verbs** (pp 12 to 15), those whose vowel usually changes in forming the imperfect indicative (→**6**)

● **Weak verbs** (pp 8 to 11), which are usually completely regular and have no vowel changes. Their endings differ from those of strong verbs (→**7**)

● **Mixed verbs** (pp 16 and 17), which have a vowel change like strong verbs, but the endings of weak verbs (→**8**)

Continued

1 ich hole
I fetch, I am fetching, I do fetch

2 ich holte
I fetched, I was fetching, I used to fetch

3 (daß) ich hole
(that) I fetch/I fetched

4 (daß) ich holte
(that) I fetched

5 ich hole	I fetch
wir holen	we fetch
du holtest	you fetched
6 singen	to sing
er singt	he sings
er sang	he sang
7 holen	to fetch
er holt	he fetches
er holte	he fetched
8 nennen	to name
er nennt	he names
er nannte	he named

Weak Verbs

Weak verbs are usually **regular** in conjugation. Their simple tenses are formed as follows:

- **Present** and **imperfect** tenses are formed by adding the endings shown below to the verb **stem**. This stem is formed by removing the **-en** ending of the infinitive (the form found in the dictionary) (→**1**)

- Where the infinitive of a weak verb ends in **-eln** or **-ern**, only the **-n** is removed to form the verb stem (→**2**)

- The endings are as follows (→**3**):

	PRESENT INDICATIVE	PRESENT SUBJUNCTIVE
1st singular	**-e**	**-e**
2nd	**-st**	**-est**
3rd	**-t**	**-e**
1st plural	**-en**	**-en**
2nd	**-t**	**-et**
3rd	**-en**	**-en**

	IMPERFECT INDICATIVE	IMPERFECT SUBJUNCTIVE
1st singular	**-te**	**-te**
2nd	**-test**	**-test**
3rd	**-te**	**-te**
1st plural	**-ten**	**-ten**
2nd	**-tet**	**-tet**
3rd	**-ten**	**-ten**

Continued

1 *INFINITIVE*   *STEM*

holen	to fetch	**hol-**
machen	to make	**mach-**
kauen	to chew	**kau-**

2		
wandern	to roam	**wander-**
handeln	to trade,	**handel-**
	to act	

3 **holen**   to fetch

PRESENT INDICATIVE	*PRESENT SUBJUNCTIVE*	
ich hole	ich hole	I fetch
du holst	du holest	you fetch
er/sie/es holt	er/sie/es hole	he/she/it fetches
wir holen	wir holen	we fetch
ihr holt	ihr holet	you (*plural*) fetch
sie/Sie holen	sie/Sie holen	they/you (*polite*) fetch

IMPERFECT INDICATIVE AND SUBJUNCTIVE
(*These tenses are identical for weak verbs*)

ich holte	I fetched
du holtest	you fetched
er/sie/es holte	he/she/it fetched
wir holten	we fetched
ihr holtet	you (*plural*) fetched
sie/Sie holten	they/you (*polite*) fetched

Weak Verbs (contd)

- Where the stem of a weak verb ends in **-d** or **-t**, an extra **-e-** is inserted before those endings where this will ease pronunciation (→**1**)

- Weak verbs whose stems end in **-m** or **-n** may take this extra **-e-**, or not, depending on whether its addition is necessary for pronunciation. If the **-m** or **-n** is preceded by a consonant *other than* **l, r** or **h**, the **-e-** is inserted (→**2**)

- Weak (and strong) verbs whose stem ends in a sibilant sound (**-s, -z, -ß**) normally lose the **-s-** of the second person singular ending (the **du** form) in the present indicative (→**3**)

  NOTE: When this sibilant is **-sch**, the **-s-** of the ending remains (→**4**)

1   **reden**   to speak   **arbeiten**   to work

PRESENT	IMPERFECT	PRESENT	IMPERFECT
ich rede	ich redete	ich arbeite	ich arbeitete
du redest	du redetest	du arbeitest	du arbeitetest
er redet	er redete	er arbeitet	er arbeitete
wir reden	wir redeten	wir arbeiten	wir arbeiteten
ihr redet	ihr redetet	ihr arbeitet	ihr arbeitetet
sie reden	sie redeten	sie arbeiten	sie arbeiteten

2   **atmen**   to breathe   **segnen**   to bless

PRESENT	IMPERFECT	PRESENT	IMPERFECT
ich atme	ich atmete	ich segne	ich segnete
du atmest	du atmetest	du segnest	du segnetest
er atmet	er atmete	er segnet	er segnete
wir atmen	wir atmeten	wir segnen	wir segneten
ihr atmet	ihr atmetet	ihr segnet	ihr segnetet
sie atmen	sie atmeten	sie segnen	sie segneten

BUT:

umarmen   to embrace   **lernen**   to learn

PRESENT	IMPERFECT	PRESENT	IMPERFECT
ich umarme	ich umarmte	ich lerne	ich lernte
du umarmst	du umarmtest	du lernst	du lerntest
er umarmt	er umarmte	er lernt	er lernte
wir umarmen	wir umarmten	wir lernen	wir lernten
ihr umarmt	ihr umarmtet	ihr lernt	ihr lerntet
sie umarmen	sie umarmten	sie lernen	sie lernten

3   **grüßen**   to greet   **4**   **löschen**   to extinguish

PRESENT	PRESENT
ich grüße	ich lösche
du **grüßt**	du löschst
er grüßt	er löscht
wir grüßen	wir löschen
ihr grüßt	ihr löscht
sie grüßen	sie löschen

Strong Verbs

A list of the most useful strong verbs is given on pp 86 to 97.

- What differentiates strong verbs from weak ones is that when forming their **imperfect indicative** tense, strong verbs undergo a vowel change and have a different set of endings (→**1**)

  Their past participles are also formed differently (see p 24).

- To form the **imperfect subjunctive** of strong verbs, the endings from the appropriate table below are added to the stem of the imperfect indicative, but the vowel is modified by an umlaut where this is possible, i.e. **a → ä, o → ö, u → ü**. Exceptions to this are clearly shown in the table of strong verbs (→**2**)

The endings for the simple tenses of strong verbs are as follows (→**3**)

	PRESENT INDICATIVE	PRESENT SUBJUNCTIVE
1st singular	**-e**	**-e**
2nd	**-st**	**-est**
3rd	**-t**	**-e**
1st plural	**-en**	**-en**
2nd	**-t**	**-et**
3rd	**-en**	**-en**
	IMPERFECT INDICATIVE	IMPERFECT SUBJUNCTIVE
1st singular	—	**-e**
2nd	**-st**	**-(e)st**
3rd	—	**-e**
1st plural	**-en**	**-en**
2nd	**-t**	**-(e)t**
3rd	**-en**	**-en**

Continued

1 Compare:

	INFINITIVE	*PRESENT*	*IMPERFECT*
WEAK	**sagen** to say	**er sagt**	**er sagte**
STRONG	**rufen** to shout	**er ruft**	**er rief**

2

	IMPERFECT INDICATIVE	*IMPERFECT SUBJUNCTIVE*
	er gab he gave	**er gäbe** (*umlaut added*)
BUT	**er rief** he shouted	**er riefe** (*no umlaut possible*)

3 singen to sing

PRESENT INDICATIVE	*PRESENT SUBJUNCTIVE*
ich sing**e**	ich sing**e**
du sing**st**	du sing**est**
er sing**t**	er sing**e**
wir sing**en**	wir sing**en**
ihr sing**t**	ihr sing**et**
sie sing**en**	sie sing**en**
Sie sing**en**	Sie sing**en**

IMPERFECT INDICATIVE	*IMPERFECT SUBJUNCTIVE*
ich sang	ich säng**e**
du sang**st**	du säng**(e)st**
er sang	er säng**e**
wir sang**en**	wir säng**en**
ihr sang**t**	ihr säng**(e)t**
sie sang**en**	sie säng**en**
Sie sang**en**	Sie säng**en**

Strong Verbs (contd)

- In the present tense of strong verbs, the vowel also often changes for the second and third persons singular (the **du** and **er/sie/es** forms).
  The pattern of possible changes is as follows:

  long **e** → **ie**
  short **e** → **i**
  a → **ä**
  au → **äu**
  o → **ö**

  Verbs which undergo these changes are clearly shown in the table on p 86 (→**1**)

- Strong (and weak) verbs whose stem ends with a sibilant sound (**-s, -z, -ß**) normally lose the **-s-** of the second person singular ending (the **du** form) in the *present indicative*, unless the sibilant is **-sch**, when it remains (→**2**)

- In the second person singular of the *imperfect* tense of strong verbs whose stem ends in a sibilant sound (including **-sch**) the sibilant remains, and an **-e-** is inserted between it and the appropriate ending (→**3**)

1   **sehen** to see   **helfen** to help
   ich sehe   ich helfe
   du siehst   du hilfst
   er/sie/es sieht   er/sie/es hilft
   wir sehen   wir helfen
   ihr seht   ihr helft
   sie sehen   sie helfen

   fahren to drive   **saufen** to booze   **stoßen** to push
   ich fahre   ich saufe   ich stoße
   du fährst   du säufst   du stößt
   er fährt   er säuft   er stößt
   wir fahren   wir saufen   wir stoßen
   ihr fahrt   ihr sauft   ihr stoßt
   sie fahren   sie saufen   sie stoßen

2   **wachsen** to grow   **waschen** to wash
   ich wachse   ich wasche
   du wächst   du wäschst
   er wächst   er wäscht
   wir wachsen   wir waschen
   ihr wachst   ihr wascht
   sie wachsen   sie waschen

3   **lesen** to read   **schließen** to close   **waschen** to wash
   ich las   ich schloß   ich wusch
   du lasest   du schlossest   du wuschest
   er las   er schloß   er wusch
   wir lasen   wir schlossen   wir wuschen
   ihr last   ihr schloßt   ihr wuscht
   sie lasen   sie schlossen   sie wuschen

Mixed Verbs

There are nine **mixed** verbs in German, and, as their name implies, they are formed according to a mixture of the rules already outlined for weak and strong verbs.

The mixed verbs are:

denken to think	**kennen** to know	**nennen** to name
rennen to run	**senden** to send	**bringen** to bring
brennen to burn	**wenden** to turn	**wissen** to know

Full details of their principal parts are given in the verb list beginning on p 86.

- Mixed verbs form their **imperfect** tense by adding the weak verb endings to a stem whose vowel has been changed as for a strong verb (→**1**)

  NOTE: **bringen** and **denken** have a consonant change too in their imperfect forms (→**2**)

- The **imperfect subjunctive** forms of mixed verbs are unusual and should be noted (→**3**)

- Other tenses of mixed verbs are formed as for strong verbs.

- The past participle of mixed verbs has characteristics of both weak and strong verbs, as shown on p 24.

1 *IMPERFECT INDICATIVE*

kennen to know	**wissen** to know	**senden** to send
ich **kann**te	ich **wuß**te	ich **sand**te
du **kann**test	du **wuß**test	du **sand**test
er **kann**te	er **wuß**te	er **sand**te
wir **kann**ten	wir **wuß**ten	wir **sand**ten
ihr **kann**tet	ihr **wuß**tet	ihr **sand**tet
sie **kann**ten	sie **wuß**ten	sie **sand**ten

2 *IMPERFECT INDICATIVE*

denken to think	**bringen** to bring
ich **dachte**	ich **brachte**
du **dachtest**	du **brachtest**
er **dachte**	er **brachte**
wir **dachten**	wir **brachten**
ihr **dachtet**	ihr **brachtet**
sie **dachten**	sie **brachten**

3 *IMPERFECT SUBJUNCTIVE*

kennen	**rennen**	**senden**
ich kennte	ich rennte	ich sendete
du kenntest	du renntest	du sendetest
er kennte *etc*	er rennte *etc*	er sendete *etc*
brennen	**wissen**	**wenden**
ich brennte	ich wüßte	ich wendete
du brenntest	du wüßtest	du wendetest
er brennte *etc*	er wüßte etc	er wendete *etc*
denken	**bringen**	**nennen**
ich dächte	ich brächte	ich nennte
du dächtest	du brächtest	du nenntest
er dächte *etc*	er brächte *etc*	er nennte *etc*

The Imperative

This is the form of a verb used to give an order or a command, or to make a request:

Come here/stand up/please bring me a beer   (→1)

- German has three main imperative forms. These go with the three ways of addressing people **Sie**, **du** and **ihr** (see p 160)

	FORMATION	EXAMPLES	
SINGULAR	stem (+ e)	**hol(e)!**	*fetch!*
PLURAL	stem + **t**	**holt!**	*fetch!*
POLITE (*sing* and *pl*)	stem + **en Sie**	**holen Sie!**	*fetch!*

- The **-e** of the singular form is often dropped, BUT NOT where the verb stem ends in **-t**, **-d**, **-chn**, **-ckn**, **-dn**, **-fn**, **-gn** or **-tm** (→2)

- **Weak verbs** ending in **-eln** or **-ern** take the **-e** ending in the singular form, but the additional **-e-** within the stem may be dropped (→3)

- Any vowel change in the present tense of a **strong verb** (see p 14) occurs also in its singular imperative form and no **-e** is added (→4)

  BUT if the vowel modification in the present tense of a **strong verb** is the addition of an umlaut, this is not added in the singular form of the imperative (→5)

- In the imperative form of a **reflexive verb** (see p 30) the pronoun is placed immediately after the verb (→6)

- **Separable prefixes** (see p 72) are placed at the end of an imperative statement (→7)

Continued

1   *SINGULAR*:   **Komm mal her!**   Come here!
    PLURAL: **Steht auf!**   Stand up!
    POLITE: **Kommen Sie herein!**   Do come in

2   **Hör zu!** Listen!
    Hol es! Fetch it!
    BUT:
    Arbeite tüchtig! Work hard!

3   **wandern**   to walk   **handeln**   to act
    wand(e)re! walk!   **hand(e)le!** act!

4   **nehmen**   to take   **helfen**   to help
    du nimmst you take   **du hilfst** you help
    nimm! take!   **hilf!** help!

    EXCEPTION:
    sehen   to see
    sieh(e)!   see!

5   **laufen**   to run   **stoßen**   to push
    du läufst you run   **du stößt** you push
    lauf(e)! run!   **stoß(e)!** push!

6   **sich setzen** to sit down:
    Setz dich!
    Setzt euch!
    Setzen Sie sich!

7   **zumachen** to close: **aufhören** to stop:
    Mach die Tür zu!   **Hör aber endlich auf!**
    Close the door!   Do stop it!

The Imperative (contd)

- Imperatives are followed in German by an exclamation mark, unless the imperative is not intended as a command (→**1**)

- **du** and **ihr**, though not normally present in imperative forms, may be included for emphasis (→**2**)

- An imperative form also exists for the **wir** form of the verb. It consists of the normal present tense form, but with the pronoun **wir** *following* the verb. It is used for making suggestions (→**3**)

- The imperative forms of **sein** (*to be*) are irregular (→**4**)

- The particles **auch, nur, mal, doch** are frequently used with imperatives. They heighten or soften the imperative effect, or add a note of encouragement to a request or command. Often they have no direct equivalent in English and are therefore not always translated (→**5**)

Some Alternatives to the Imperative in German

- Infinitives are often used instead of the imperative in written instructions or public announcements (→**6**)

- The impersonal passive (see p 34) may be used (→**7**)

- Nouns, adjectives or adverbs can also be used with imperative effect (→**8**)
  Some of these have become set expressions (→**9**)

1 **Laß ihn in Ruhe!** Leave him alone
  Sagen Sie mir bitte, wie spät es ist What's the time please?

2 **Geht ihr voran!** You go on ahead
  Sag du ihm, was los ist You tell him what's wrong

3 **Nehmen wir an, daß ...**
  Let's assume that ...
  Sagen wir mal, es habe 4,000 DM gekostet
  Let's just say it cost 4,000 marks

4 **sein** to be
  sei!
  seid!
  seien wir!
  seien Sie!

5 **Geh doch!** Go on!/Get going!
  Sag mal, ... Tell me ...
  Versuchen Sie es mal! Do give it a try!
  Komm schon! Do come/Please come
  Mach es auch richtig! Be sure to do it properly

6 **Einsteigen!**
  All aboard!
  Zwiebeln abziehen und in Ringe schneiden
  Peel the onions and slice them

7 **Jetzt wird aufgeräumt!**
  You're going to clear up now!

8 **Ruhe!** Be quiet! Silence!
  Vorsicht! Careful! Look out!

9 **Achtung!** Listen!/Attention!
  Rauchen verboten! No smoking

Compound Tenses

The present and imperfect tenses in German are **simple** tenses, as described on pp 6 to 17.

All other tenses, called **compound tenses**, are formed for all types of verb by using the appropriate tense of an **auxiliary verb** plus a part of the main verb.

There are three auxiliary verbs:
haben for past tenses
sein also for past tenses
werden for future and conditional tenses

The **compound past tenses** in German are:

Perfect indicative   (→**1**)
Perfect subjunctive   (→**2**)
Pluperfect indicative   (→**3**)
Pluperfect subjunctive   (→**4**)

These are dealt with on pp 26 ff.

The **future** and **conditional tenses** in German are all compound tenses. They are:

Future indicative   (→**5**)
Future subjunctive   (→**6**)
Future perfect   (→**7**)
Conditional   (→**8**)
Conditional perfect   (→**9**)

These are dealt with on pp 28 ff.

	with **haben**	with **sein**
1	**er hat geholt** he (has) fetched	**er ist gereist** he (has) travelled
2	**er habe geholt** he (has) fetched	**er sei gereist** he (has) travelled
3	**er hatte geholt** he had fetched	**er war gereist** he had travelled
4	**er hätte geholt** he had fetched	**er wäre gereist** he had travelled
5	**er wird holen** he will fetch	**er wird reisen** he will travel
6	**er werde holen** he will fetch	**er werde reisen** he will travel
7	**er wird geholt haben** he will have fetched	**er wird gereist sein** he will have travelled
8	**er würde holen** he would fetch	**er würde reisen** he would travel
9	**er würde geholt haben** he would have fetched	**er würde gereist sein** he would have travelled

Compound Past Tenses: Formation

- Compound past tenses are normally formed by using the auxiliary verb **haben**, plus the past participle of the main verb (see below) (→**1**)

- Certain types of verb take **sein** instead of **haben**, and this is clearly indicated in the verb tables starting on p 86. They fall into three main types:
  1. intransitive verbs (those that take no direct object, often showing a change of state or place) (→**2**)
  2. certain verbs meaning "to happen" (→**3**)
  3. miscellaneous others, including:
     bleiben to remain, **gelingen** to succeed
     begegnen to meet, **sein** to be
     werden to become (→**4**)

- In some cases the verb can be conjugated with either **haben** or **sein**, depending on whether it is used transitively (with a direct object) or intransitively (where no direct object is possible) (→**5**)

The Past Participle: Formation (see also p 50)

- **Weak** verbs add the prefix **ge-** and the suffix **-t** to the verb stem (→**6**)

  Verbs ending in **-ieren** or **-eien** omit the **ge-** (→**7**)

- **Strong** verbs add the prefix **ge-** and the suffix **-en** to the verb stem (→**8**). The vowel of the stem may be modified (see verb list, p 86) (→**9**)

- **Mixed** verbs add the prefix **ge-** and the "weak" suffix **-t** to the stem. The stem vowel is modified as for many strong verbs (→**10**)

Continued

1 Haben Sie gut geschlafen?
Did you sleep well?
Die Kinder hatten fleißig gearbeitet
The children had worked hard

2 Wir sind nach Bonn gefahren
We went to Bonn
Er ist schnell eingeschlafen
He quickly fell asleep

3 Was ist geschehen?
What happened?

4 Er ist zu Hause geblieben   **Er ist krank gewesen**
He stayed at home   He has been ill
Es ist uns nicht gelungen   **Sie ist krank geworden**
We did not succeed   She became ill
Er ist einem Freund begegnet
He met a friend

5 Er hat den Wagen nach Köln gefahren
He drove the car to Cologne
Er ist nach Köln gefahren
He went to Cologne

6 holen to fetch   **9 singen** to sing
  geholt fetched   **gesungen** sung

7 studieren to study   **10 senden** to send
  studiert studied   **gesandt** sent
  prophezeien to prophesy   **bringen** to bring
  prophezeit prophesied   **gebracht** brought

8 laufen to run
  gelaufen run

For a full list of strong and mixed verbs see p 86

Compound Past Tenses: Formation (contd)

The formation of past participles for weak, strong and mixed verbs is described on p 24, and a comprehensive list of the principal parts of the most commonly used strong and mixed verbs is provided for reference on pp 86 to 97.

How to form the compound past tenses:

Perfect indicative	the present tense of **haben** or **sein** plus the past participle of the verb (→1)
Perfect subjunctive	(used in indirect or reported speech) the present subjunctive of **haben** or **sein** plus the past participle (→2)
Pluperfect indicative	imperfect indicative of **haben** or **sein** plus the past participle (→3)
Pluperfect subjunctive	(for indirect or reported speech) imperfect subjunctive of **haben** or **sein** plus the past participle (→4)

NOTE: The pluperfect subjunctive is a frequently used tense in German, since it can replace the much clumsier conditional perfect tense shown on p 28 with **haben**   with **sein**

1 *PERFECT INDICATIVE*

ich habe geholt   ich bin gereist
du hast geholt   du bist gereist
er/sie/es hat geholt   er/sie/es ist gereist
wir haben geholt   wir sind gereist
ihr habt geholt   ihr seid gereist
sie/Sie haben geholt   sie/Sie sind gereist

2 *PERFECT SUBJUNCTIVE*

ich habe geholt   ich sei gereist
du habest geholt   du sei(e)st gereist
er/sie/es habe geholt   er/sie/es sei gereist
wir haben geholt   wir seien gereist
ihr habet geholt   ihr seiet gereist
sie/Sie haben geholt   sie/Sie seien gereist

3 *PLUPERFECT INDICATIVE*

ich hatte geholt   ich war gereist
du hattest geholt   du warst gereist
er/sie/es hatte geholt   er/sie/es war gereist
wir hatten geholt   wir waren gereist
ihr hattet geholt   ihr wart gereist
sie/Sie hatten geholt   sie/Sie waren gereist

4 *PLUPERFECT SUBJUNCTIVE*

ich hätte geholt   ich wäre gereist
du hättest geholt   du wär(e)st gereist
er/sie/es hätte geholt   er/sie/es wäre gereist
wir hätten geholt   wir wären gereist
ihr hättet geholt   ihr wär(e)t gereist
sie/Sie hätten geholt   sie/Sie wären gereist

Future and Conditional Tenses: Formation

- The **future** and **conditional** tenses are formed in the same way for all verbs, whether weak, strong or mixed.

- The auxiliary **werden** is used for all verbs together with the infinitive of the main verb.

- The infinitive is usually placed at the end of the clause (see p 224).

How to form the future and conditional tenses:

Future indicative	present tense of **werden** plus the infinitive of the verb (→**1**)
Future subjunctive	present subjunctive of **werden** plus the infinitive (→**2**)
Future perfect	present indicative of **werden** plus the **perfect infinitive** (see below) (→**3**)
Conditional	imperfect subjunctive of **werden** plus the infinitive (→**4**)
Conditional perfect	imperfect subjunctive of **werden** plus the perfect infinitive (see below) (→**5**)
	NOTE: often replaced by the pluperfect subjunctive

- The **perfect infinitive** consists of the infinitive of **haben/sein** plus the past participle of the verb.

1 *FUTURE INDICATIVE*
ich werde holen   **wir werden holen**
du wirst holen   **ihr werdet holen**
er/sie/es wird holen   **sie/Sie werden holen**

2 *FUTURE SUBJUNCTIVE*
ich werde holen   **wir werden holen**
du werdest holen   **ihr werdet holen**
er/sie/es werde holen   **sie/Sie werden holen**

3 *FUTURE PERFECT*
ich werde geholt haben   **wir werden geholt haben**
du wirst geholt haben   **ihr werdet geholt haben**
er wird geholt haben   **sie/Sie werden geholt haben**

4 *CONDITIONAL*
ich würde holen   **wir würden holen**
du würdest holen   **ihr würdet holen**
er/sie/es würde holen   **sie/Sie würden holen**

5 *CONDITIONAL PERFECT*[1]
ich würde geholt haben   **wir würden geholt haben**
du würdest geholt haben   **ihr würdet geholt haben**
er würde geholt haben   **sie/Sie würden geholt haben**

1. *NB Often replaced by the pluperfect subjunctive (see p 26)*

Reflexive Verbs

A verb whose action is reflected back to its subject may be termed reflexive: *she* washes *herself*.
Reflexive verbs in German are recognized in the infinitive by the preceding reflexive pronoun **sich** (→**1**)
German has many reflexive verbs, a great number of which are not reflexive in English (→**1**)

- Reflexive verbs are composed of the verb and a reflexive pronoun (see p 170).
  This pronoun may be either the direct object (and therefore in the accusative case) or the indirect object (and therefore in the dative case) (→**2**)

- Many verbs in German which are not essentially reflexive may become reflexive by the addition of a reflexive pronoun (→**3**)
  When a verb with an indirect object is made reflexive (see p 170) the pronoun is usually dative (→**4**)

- A direct object reflexive pronoun changes to the dative if another direct object is present (→**5**)

- In a main clause the reflexive pronoun follows the verb (→**6**)
  After inversion (see p 226), or in a subordinate clause, the reflexive pronoun must come after the subject if the subject is a personal pronoun (→**7**)
  It may precede or follow a noun subject (→**8**)

- Reflexive verbs are always conjugated with **haben** *except* where the pronoun is used to mean *each other*. Then the verb is normally conjugated with **sein**.

- The imperative forms are show on p 19.

Continued

1 sich **beeilen** to hurry
   wir beeilen uns we are hurrying

2 sich (*accusative*) erinnern   sich (*dative*) erlauben
   to remember   to allow oneself
   ich erinnere mich   **ich erlaube mir**
   du erinnerst dich   **du erlaubst dir**
   er/sie/es erinnert sich   **er/sie/es erlaubt sich**
   wir erinnern uns   **wir erlauben uns**
   ihr erinnert euch   **ihr erlaubt euch**
   sie/Sie erinnern sich   **sie/Sie erlauben sich**

3 **etwas melden** to report something
   sich **melden** to report for/to volunteer for
   Ich habe mich gemeldet I volunteered
4 **weh tun** to hurt
   sich **weh tun** to get hurt
   Hast du dir weh getan? Have you hurt yourself?
   kaufen to buy
   Er kaufte ihr einen Mantel He bought her a coat
   Er kaufte sich (*dative*) einen neuen Mantel
   He bought himself a new coat
5 **Ich wasche mich** I am having a wash
   Ich wasche mir die Hände I am washing my hands
6 **Er wird sich darüber freuen**
   He'll be pleased about that
7 **Darüber wird er sich freuen**
   Ich frage mich, ob er sich darüber freuen wird
   I wonder if he'll be pleased about that
8 **Langsam drehten sich die Kinder um**
   OR
   Langsam drehten die Kinder sich um
   The children slowly turned around

Reflexive Verbs (contd)

Some examples of verbs which can be used with a reflexive pronoun in the accusative case:

  sich anziehen to get dressed (→**1**)
  sich aufregen to get excited (→**2**)
  sich beeilen to hurry (→**3**)
  sich beschäftigen mit[1] to be occupied with (→**4**)
  sich bewerben um[1] to apply for (→**5**)
  sich erinnern an[1] to remember (→**6**)
  sich freuen auf[1] to look forward to (→**7**)
  sich interessieren für[1] to be interested in (→**8**)
  sich irren to be wrong (→**9**)
  sich melden to report (for duty etc)
  sich rasieren to shave
  sich (hin)setzen to sit down (→**10**)
  sich trauen[2] to trust oneself
  sich umsehen to look around (→**11**)

Some examples of verbs which can be used with a reflexive pronoun in the dative case:

  sich abgewöhnen to give up (something) (→**12**)
  sich aneignen to appropriate
  sich ansehen to have a look at
  sich einbilden to imagine (wrongly) (→**13**)
  sich erlauben to allow oneself (→**14**)
  sich leisten to treat oneself (→**15**)
  sich nähern to get close to
  sich vornehmen to plan to do (→**16**)
  sich vorstellen to imagine (→**17**)
  sich wünschen to want (→**18**)

1. For verbs normally followed by a preposition, the reader is referred to p 76 ff.
2. **trauen** when non-reflexive takes the dative case.

1 Du sollst dich sofort anziehen
You are to get dressed immediately
2 Reg dich doch nicht so auf!
Calm down!
3 Wir müssen uns beeilen
We must hurry
4 Sie beschäftigen sich sehr mit den Kindern
They spend a lot of time with the children
5 Hast du dich um diese Stelle beworben?
Have you applied for this post?
6 Ich erinnere mich nicht daran
I can't remember it
7 Ich freue mich auf die Fahrt
I am looking forward to the journey
8 Interessierst du dich für Musik?
Are you interested in music?
9 Er hat sich geirrt
He was wrong
10 Bitte, setzt euch hin!
Please sit down
11 Die Kinder sahen sich erstaunt um
The children looked around in amazement
12 Eigentlich müßte man sich das Rauchen abgewöhnen
One really ought to give up smoking
13 Bilde dir doch nichts ein!
Don't kid yourself!
14 Eins könntest du dir doch erlauben
You could surely allow yourself one
15 Wenn ich mir nur einen Mercedes leisten könnte!
If only I could afford a Mercedes!
16 Du hast dir wieder zuviel vorgenommen!
You've taken on too much again!
17 So hatte ich es mir oft vorgestellt
I had often imagined it like this
18 Was wünscht ihr euch zu Weihnachten?
What do you want for Christmas?

The Passive

In active tenses, the subject of a verb carries out the action of the verb, but in passive tenses the subject of the verb has something done to it.
Compare the following:
> *Peter kicked the cat* (subject: *Peter*)
> *The cat was kicked by Peter* (subject: *the cat*)

- English uses the verb "to be" to form its passive tenses. German uses **werden** (→**1**)
  A sample verb is conjugated in the passive on pp 39 to 41.

- In English, the word "by" usually introduces the agent through which the action of a passive tense is performed. In German this agent is introduced by:
  > **von** for the performer of the action
  > **durch** for an inanimate cause (→**2**)

- The passive can be used to add impersonality or distance to an event (→**3**)
  It may also be used where the identity of the cause of the deed is unknown or not important (→**4**)

- In general however the passive is used less in German than in English. The following are common replacements for the passive:

  1. an active tense with the impersonal pronoun **man** as subject (meaning *they/one*). This resembles the use of *on* in French, and **man** is not always translated as *one* or *they* (→**5**)

  2. **sich lassen** plus a verb in the infinitive (→**6**)

Continued

1 Das Auto wurde gekauft
The car was bought

2 Das ist von seinem Onkel geschickt worden
It was sent by his uncle
Das Kind wurde von einem Hund gebissen
The child was bitten by a dog
Seine Bewerbung ist von der Firma abgelehnt worden
(*the firm is viewed as a human agent*)
His application was turned down by the firm

Die Tür wurde durch den Wind geöffnet
The door was opened by the wind
Das Getreide wurde durch den Sturm niedergeschlagen
The crop was flattened by the storm

3 Die Praxis ist von Dr. Disselkamp übernommen worden
The practice has been taken over by Dr Disselkamp
Anfang 1993 wurde ein weiterer Anschlag auf sein Leben gemacht
Another attempt was made on his life early in 1993

4 In letzter Zeit sind neue Gesetze eingeführt worden
New laws have recently been introduced

5 Man hatte es schon verkauft
It had already been sold
Man wird es verkauft haben
It will have been sold

6 Das läßt sich schnell herausfinden
We'll/You'll/One will be able to find that out quickly

The Passive (contd)

- In English the indirect object of an active tense can become the subject of a passive statement e.g.

   Peter gave *him* a car (*him* = to him)

   He was given a car by Peter

   This is not possible in German, where the indirect object (*him*) must remain in the dative case (see p 110). There are two ways of handling this in German:

   1. with the direct object (*car*) as the subject of a passive verb (→**1**)
   2. by means of an impersonal passive construction, with or without the impersonal subject **es** (→**1**)

   These constructions would however normally be avoided in favour of an active tense, when the agent of the action is known (→**2**)

- Verbs which are normally followed by the dative case in German and so have only an indirect object (see p 80) should therefore be especially noted, as they can only adopt the impersonal or **man**-forms of the passive (→**3**)

- Some passive tenses are avoided in German, as they are inelegant (and difficult to use!). For instance, the future perfect passives should be replaced by an active tense or a **man**-construction (→**4**)

   The conditional perfect passives are also rarely used, past conditional being shown by the pluperfect subjunctives, either passive or active (→**5**)

- English passive constructions such as

   he was heard whistling/they were thought to be dying

   are not possible in German (→**6**)

Continued

1 Ein Auto wurde ihm von Peter geschenkt
OR:
Es wurde ihm von Peter ein Auto geschenkt
OR:
Ihm wurde von Peter ein Auto geschenkt
He was given a car by Peter

2 Peter schenkte ihm ein Auto
Peter gave him a car

3 helfen (+ *dative*)   to help:
Sie half mir   **Mir wurde von ihr geholfen**
She helped me   →   *OR*:
                         Es wurde mir von ihr geholfen
                         I was helped by her

4 Er meint, es werde schon gesehen worden sein
He thinks that it will already have been seen

BETTER: **Er meint, man werde es schon gesehen haben**

5 Es würde geholt worden sein / Man würde es geholt haben
It would have been fetched

BETTER: **Es wäre geholt worden / Man hätte es geholt**

6 Man hörte ihn singen
He was heard singing
Man sah sie ankommen
She was seen arriving
Man glaubte, er sei betrunken
He was thought to be drunk

Passive Tenses: Conjugation

Simple Tenses

Present passive indicative
e.g. *it is seen*

present indicative of **werden** + past participle of the verb (→**1**)

Present passive subjunctive

present subjunctive of **werden** + past participle of the verb (→**2**)

Imperfect passive indicative
e.g. *it was seen*

imperfect indicative of **werden** + past participle of the verb (→**3**)

Imperfect passive subjunctive

imperfect subjunctive of **werden** + past participle of the verb (→**4**)

Compound Tenses

Perfect passive indicative
e.g. *it has been seen*

present indicative of **sein** + past participle of the verb + **worden** (→**5**)

Perfect passive subjunctive

present subjunctive of **sein** + past participle of the verb + **worden** (→**6**)

Pluperfect passive indicative
e.g. *it had been seen*

imperfect indicative of **sein** + past participle + **worden** (→**7**)

Continued

1 *PRESENT PASSIVE INDICATIVE*

ich werde gesehen	**wir werden gesehen**
du wirst gesehen	**ihr werdet gesehen**
er/sie/es wird gesehen	**sie/Sie werden gesehen**

OR: **man sieht mich/man sieht dich** *etc*

2 *PRESENT PASSIVE SUBJUNCTIVE*

ich werde gesehen	**wir werden gesehen**
du werdest gesehen	**ihr werdet gesehen**
er/sie/es werde gesehen	**sie/Sie werden gesehen**

OR: **man sehe mich/man sehe dich** *etc*

3 *IMPERFECT PASSIVE INDICATIVE*

ich wurde gesehen/wir wurden gesehen *etc*

OR: **man sah mich/man sah uns** *etc*

4 *IMPERFECT PASSIVE SUBJUNCTIVE*

ich würde gesehen/wir würden gesehen *etc*

OR: **man sähe mich/man sähe uns** *etc*

5 *PERFECT PASSIVE INDICATIVE*

ich bin gesehen worden/wir sind gesehen worden *etc*

OR: **man hat mich/uns gesehen** *etc*

6 *PERFECT PASSIVE SUBJUNCTIVE*

ich sei gesehen worden/wir seien gesehen worden *etc*

OR: **man habe mich/uns gesehen** *etc*

7 *PLUPERFECT PASSIVE INDICATIVE*

ich war gesehen worden/wir waren gesehen worden *etc*

OR: **man hatte mich/uns gesehen** *etc*

Passive Tenses: Conjugation (contd)

Pluperfect passive subjunctive	imperfect subjunctive of **sein** + past participle of the verb + **worden** (→**1**)
Present passive infinitive e.g. *to be seen*	infinitive of **werden** + past participle of the verb (→**2**)
Future passive indicative e.g. *it will be seen*	present indicative of **werden** + present passive infinitive of the verb (→**3**)
Future passive subjunctive	present subjunctive of **werden** + present passive infinitive (→**4**)
Perfect passive infinitive e.g. *to have been seen*	past participle of the verb + **worden sein** (→**5**)
Future perfect passive e.g. *it will have been seen*	present indicative of **werden** + perfect passive infinitive of the verb (→**6**)
Conditional passive e.g. *it would be seen*	imperfect subjunctive of **werden** + present passive infinitive of the verb (→**7**)
Conditional perfect passive e.g. *it would have been seen*	imperfect subjunctive of **werden** + perfect passive infinitive of the verb (→**8**)

1 *PLUPERFECT PASSIVE SUBJUNCTIVE*
ich wäre gesehen worden/wir wären gesehen worden *etc*

OR: **man hätte mich/uns gesehen** *etc*

2 *PRESENT PASSIVE INFINITIVE*
gesehen werden

3 *FUTURE PASSIVE INDICATIVE*
ich werde gesehen werden/wir werden gesehen werden *etc*

OR: **man wird mich/uns sehen** *etc*

4 *FUTURE PASSIVE SUBJUNCTIVE*
ich werde gesehen werden/wir werden gesehen werden *etc*

OR: **man werde mich/uns sehen** *etc*

5 *PERFECT PASSIVE INFINITIVE*
gesehen worden sein

6 *FUTURE PERFECT PASSIVE*
ich werde/wir werden gesehen worden sein *etc*

OR: **man wird mich/uns gesehen haben** *etc*

7 *CONDITIONAL PASSIVE*
ich würde gesehen werden/wir würden gesehen werden

OR: **man würde mich/uns sehen** *etc*

8 *CONDITIONAL PERFECT PASSIVE*
ich würde/wir würden gesehen worden sein

OR: **man würde mich/uns gesehen haben** *etc*
OR: pluperfect subjunctive: **man hätte mich/uns gesehen** *etc*

Impersonal Verbs

These verbs are used only in the third person singular, usually with the subject **es** meaning *it* (→**1**)

- Intransitive verbs (verbs with no direct object) are often made impersonal in the passive to describe activity of a general nature (→**2**)

  When the verb and subject are inverted (see p 226), the **es** is omitted (→**3**)

  Impersonal verbs in the passive can also be used as an imperative form (see p 20) (→**4**)

- In certain expressions in the active, the impersonal pronoun **es** can be omitted. In this case, a personal pronoun object begins the clause (→**5**)

  In the following lists * indicates that **es** may be omitted in this way:

Some common impersonal verbs and expressions

es donnert *it's thundering*
es fällt mir ein, daß/zu* *it occurs to me that/to* (→**6**)
es fragt sich, ob *one wonders whether* (→**7**)
es freut mich, daß/zu *I am glad that/to* (→**8**)
es friert *it is freezing* (→**9**)
es gefällt mir *I like it* (→**10**)
es geht mir gut/schlecht *I'm fine/not too good*
es geht nicht *it's not possible*
es geht um *it's about*
es gelingt mir (, zu) *I succeed (in)* (→**11**)
es geschieht *it happens* (→**12**)
es gießt *it's pouring*
es handelt sich um *it's a question of*

Continued

1 **Es regnet** It's raining

2 **Es wurde viel gegessen und getrunken**
There was a lot of eating and drinking

3 **Auf der Hochzeit wurde viel gegessen und getrunken**
There was a lot of eating and drinking at the wedding

4 **Jetzt wird gearbeitet!** Now you're/we're going to work

5 **Mir ist warm** I'm warm

6 **Nachher fiel (es) mir ein, daß der Mann ziemlich komisch angezogen war**
Afterwards it occurred to me that the man was rather oddly dressed

7 **Es fragt sich, ob es sich lohnt, das zu machen**
One wonders if that's worth doing

8 **Es freut mich sehr, daß du gekommen bist**
I'm so pleased that you have come

9 **Heute nacht hat es gefroren**
It was below freezing last night

10 **Ihm hat es gar nicht gefallen**
He didn't like it at all

11 **Es war ihnen gelungen, die letzten Karten zu kriegen**
They had succeeded in getting the last tickets

12 **Und so geschah es, daß ...**
And so it came about that ...

Impersonal Verbs and Expressions (contd)

es hängt davon ab *it depends*

es hat keinen Zweck (zu) *there's no point (in)* (→**1**)

es interessiert mich, daß/zu* *I am interested that/to*

es ist mir egal (ob)* *it's all the same to me (if)* (→**2**)

es ist möglich (, daß) *it's possible (that)* (→**3**)

es ist nötig *it's necessary* (→**4**)

es ist mir, als ob* *I feel as if*

es ist mir gut/schlecht etc zumute* *I feel good/bad etc* (→**5**)

es ist schade (, daß) *it's a pity (that)*

es ist (mir) wichtig* *it's important (to me)*

es ist mir warm/kalt* *I'm hot/cold*

es ist warm/kalt *it's (the weather is) warm/cold*

es ist zu hoffen/bedauern etc* *it is to be hoped/regretted etc*

es klingelt *someone is ringing the bell* (→**6**)

es klopft *someone's knocking*

es kommt darauf an (, ob) *it all depends (whether)*

es kommt mir vor (, als ob) *it seems to me (as if)*

es läutet *the bell is ringing* (→**7**)

es liegt an *it is because of* (→**8**)

es lohnt sich (nicht) *it's (not) worth it* (→**9**)

es macht nichts *it doesn't matter*

es macht nichts aus *it makes no difference* (→**10**)

es macht mir (keinen) Spaß (, zu) *it's (no) fun (to)* (→**11**)

es passiert *it happens* (→**12**)

es regnet *it's raining* (→**13**)

es scheint mir, daß/als ob* *it seems to me that/as if*

es schneit *it's snowing*

es stellt sich heraus, daß *it turns out that*

es stimmt (nicht), daß *it's (not) true, that*

es tut mir leid (, daß) *I'm sorry (that)*

wie geht es (dir)? *how are you?* (→**14**)

mir wird schlecht *I feel sick*

1 **Es hat keinen Zweck, weiter darüber zu diskutieren**
There's no point in discussing this any further

2 **Es ist mir egal, ob du kommst oder nicht**
I don't care if you come or not

3 **Es ist doch möglich, daß der Zug Verspätung hat**
It's always possible the train has been delayed

4 **Es wird nicht nötig sein, uns darüber zu informieren**
It won't be necessary to inform us of it

5 **Mir ist heute seltsam zumute** I feel strange today

6 **Es hat gerade geklingelt**
The bell just went/The phone just rang

7 **Es hat schon geläutet** The bell has gone

8 **Woran liegt es?** Why is that?

9 **Ich weiß nicht, ob es sich lohnt oder nicht**
I don't know if it's worth it or not

10 **Mir macht es nichts aus** It makes no difference to me
Macht es Ihnen etwas aus, wenn ... Would you mind if ...

11 **Hauptsache, es macht Spaß**
The main thing is to enjoy yourself

12 **Ihm ist bestimmt etwas passiert**
Something must have happened to him

13 **Es hat den ganzen Tag geregnet** It rained the whole day

14 **Wie geht's denn? — Danke, es geht**
How are things? — All right thank you

The Infinitive

Forms

There are four forms of the infinitive (→**1**). These forms are used in certain compound tenses (see p 28). The present active infinitive is the most widely used and is the form found in dictionaries.

Uses

● Preceded by **zu** (*to*)

1. as in English, after other verbs ("I tried *to come*") (→**2**)
2. as in English, after adjectives ("it was easy *to see*") (→**3**)
3. where the English equivalent is not always an infinitive:
   — after nouns, where English may use an "-ing" form (→**4**)
   — after **sein**, where the English equivalent may be a passive tense (→**5**)

● Without **zu**, the infinitive is used after the following:

modal verbs (→**6**)
lassen (→**7**)
heißen (→**8**)
bleiben (→**9**)
gehen (→**10**)
verbs of perception (→**11**)
NOTE: verbs of perception can also be followed by a subordinate clause beginning with **wie** or **daß**, especially if the sentence is long or involved (→**12**)

Continued

1 *INFINITIVES*:

PRESENT ACTIVE	*PERFECT ACTIVE*
holen	**geholt haben**
to fetch	to have fetched
PRESENT PASSIVE	*PERFECT PASSIVE*
geholt werden	**geholt worden sein**
to be fetched	to have been fetched

2 Ich versuchte zu kommen I tried to come

3 Es war leicht zu sehen It was easy to see

4 Ich habe nur wenig Gelegenheit, Musik zu hören
I have little opportunity to listen to music

5 Er ist zu bedauern He is to be pitied

6 Er kann schwimmen He can swim

7 Sie ließen uns warten They kept us waiting

8 Er hieß ihn kommen He bade him come

9 Er blieb sitzen He remained seated

10 Sie ging einkaufen She went shopping

11 Ich sah ihn kommen I saw him coming
Er hörte sie singen He heard her singing

12 Er sah, wie sie langsam auf und ab schlenderte
He watched her strolling slowly up and down

The Infinitive (contd)

Used as an imperative
● The infinitive can be used as an imperative (see p 20) (→**1**)

Used as a noun
● The infinitive can be made into a noun by giving it a capital letter. Its gender is always neuter (→**2**)

Used with modal verbs (*see p 52*)
● An infinitive used with a modal verb is always placed at the end of a clause (see p 56) (→**3**)

● If the modal verb is in a compound tense, its auxiliary will follow the subject in a main clause in the normal way, and the modal participle comes after the infinitive. *BUT* in a subordinate clause, the auxiliary immediately precedes the infinitive and the modal participle, instead of coming at the end (→**4**)

● An infinitive expressing change of place may be omitted entirely after a modal verb (see p 56) (→**5**)

Used in infinitive phrases
Infinitive phrases can be formed with:

> **zu**   **ohne ... zu**
> **um ... zu**   **anstatt ... zu** (→**6**)

● The infinitive comes at the end of its phrase (→**7**)

● In separable verbs, **zu** is inserted *between* the verb and its prefix in the present infinitive (→**8**)

● A reflexive pronoun comes first, immediately following an introductory word if there is one (→**9**)

1 Einsteigen und Türen schließen!
All aboard! Close the doors!

2 rauchen to smoke:
Er hat das Rauchen aufgegeben
He's given up smoking

3 Wir müssen morgen einkaufen gehen
We have to go shopping tomorrow

4 Sie haben gestern aufräumen müssen
They had to tidy up yesterday
BUT
Da sie gestern haben aufräumen müssen, durften sie nicht kommen
They couldn't come as they had to tidy up yesterday

5 Er will jetzt nach Hause He wants to go home now

6 es zu tun to do it
es getan zu haben to have done it
um es zu tun in order to do it
um es getan zu haben in order to have done it
ohne es zu tun without doing it
ohne es getan zu haben without having done it
anstatt es zu tun instead of doing it
anstatt es getan zu haben instead of having done it

7 Ohne ein Wort zu sagen, verließ er das Haus
He left the house without saying a word
Er ging nach Hause, ohne mit ihr gesprochen zu haben
He went home without having spoken to her

8 aufgeben to give up:
um es aufzugeben in order to give it up

9 Sie gingen weg, ohne sich zu verabschieden
They left without saying goodbye

The Present Participle

- The present participle for all verbs is formed by adding **-d** to the infinitive form (→**1**)

- The present participle may be used as an adjective.
  As with all adjectives, it is declined if used attributively (see p 140) (→**2**)

- The present participle may also be used as an adjectival noun (see p 148) (→**3**)

The Past Participle

- For weak verbs, the past participle is formed by prefixing **ge-** and adding **-t** to the verb stem (→**4**)

- For strong verbs, the past participle is formed by adding the prefix **ge-** and the ending **-en** to the verb stem (→**5**)
  The vowel is often modified too (→**6**)
  (See list of strong and mixed verbs beginning on p 86)

- Mixed verbs form their past participle by adding the **ge-** and **-t** of weak verbs, but they change their vowel as for strong verbs. (See list, p 86) (→**7**)

- The past participles of *separable* verbs are formed according to the above rules and are joined on to the separable prefix (→**8**)

- For *inseparable* verbs, past participles are formed without the **ge-** prefix (→**9**)

- Many past participles can also be used as adjectives and adjectival nouns (→**10**)

1 **lachen** to laugh
lachend laughing

singen to sing
singend singing

2 **ein lachendes Kind** a laughing child
mit klopfendem Herzen with beating heart

3 **der Vorsitzende/ein Vorsitzender** the/a chairman

4 **machen** to do/make
gemacht done/made

5 **sehen** to see
gesehen seen

6 **singen** to sing
gesungen sung

7 **wissen** to know
gewußt known

8 **aufstehen** to get up
aufgestanden got up

nachmachen to copy/imitate
nachgemacht imitated

9 **bestellen** to order
bestellt ordered

entscheiden to decide
entschieden decided

10 **seine verlorene Brille** his lost spectacles
Wir aßen Gebratenes We ate fried food

Modal Auxiliary Verbs

Modal verbs, sometimes called modal auxiliaries, are used to *modify* other verbs (to show e.g. possibility, ability, willingness, permission, necessity) much as in English:

    he *can* swim; *may* I come?; we *shouldn't* go

- In German the modal auxiliary verbs are: **dürfen, können, mögen, müssen, sollen** and **wollen**.

- Modal verbs have some important differences in their uses and in their conjugation from other verbs, and these are clearly shown on pp 86 to 97.

- Modal verbs have the following meanings:

dürfen   *to be allowed to/may* (→**1**)
    used negatively: *must not/may not* (→**2**)
    to show probability (→**3**)
    also used in some polite expressions (→**4**)

können   *to be able to, can* (→**5**)
    in its subjunctive forms:
    would be able to/could (→**6**)
    as an informal alternative to **dürfen** with the meaning: *allowed to/can* (→**7**)
    to show possibility (→**8**)

mögen   *to like/to like to* (→**9**)
    most common in its imperfect subjunctive form which expresses polite inquiry or request: *should like to/would like to* (→**10**)
    to show possibility or probability (→**11**)

Continued

1 **Darfst du mit ins Kino kommen?**
   Are you allowed to (can you) come with us to the cinema?
   Darf ich bitte mitkommen?
   May I come with you please?
   Ich dürfte schon, aber ich will nicht
   I could (would be allowed to), but I don't want to
2 **Hier darf man nicht rauchen**
   Smoking is prohibited here
3 **Das dürfte wohl das beste sein**
   That's probably the best thing
4 **Was darf es sein?**
   Can I help you?/What would you like?
5 **Wir konnten es nicht schaffen**
   We couldn't (weren't able to) do it
6 **Er könnte noch früher kommen**
   He could (would be able to) come even earlier
   Er meinte, er könne noch früher kommen
   He thought he could come earlier
   Wir könnten vielleicht morgen hinfahren?
   Perhaps we could go there tomorrow?
7 **Kann ich (darf ich) ein Eishaben?**
   Can I (may I) have an ice-cream?
8 **Wer könnte es gewesen sein?**
   Who could it have been?
   Das kann sein
   That may be so
   BUT: **Das kann nicht sein** That cannot be so
9 **Magst du Butter?**
   Do you like butter?
10 **Wir möchten bitte etwas trinken**
   We should like something to drink
   Möchtest du sie besuchen?
   Would you like to visit her?
11 **Wie alt mag sie sein?**
   How old might she be?

Modal Auxiliary Verbs (contd)

müssen *to have to/must/need to* (→**1**)
certain idiomatic uses (→**2**)

   NOTE: for *must have ...*, use the relevant tense of
   müssen + past participle of main verb + the
   auxiliary **haben** or **sein** (→**3**)
   for *don't have to/need not*, a negative form of
   brauchen (*to need*) may be used instead of
   müssen (→**4**)

sollen *ought to/should* (→**5**)
to be (supposed) to where the demand is not self-
imposed (→**6**)
to be said to be (→**7**)
as a command, either direct or indirect (→**8**)

wollen *to want/want to* (→**9**)
used as a less formal version of **mögen** to mean:
want/wish (→**10**)
to be willing to (→**11**)
to show previous intention (→**12**)
to claim or pretend (→**13**)

Continued

1 **Er hatte jeden Tag um sechs aufstehen müssen**
He had to get up at six o'clock every day
Man mußte lachen
One had to laugh/couldn't help laughing

2 **Muß das sein?** Is that really necessary?
Ein Millionär müßte man sein!
Oh to be a millionaire!
Den Film muß man gesehen haben
That film is worth seeing

3 **Es muß geregnet haben** It must have been raining
Er meinte, es müsse am vorigen Abend passiert sein
He thought it must have happened the previous evening

4 **Das brauchtest du nicht zu sagen**
You didn't have to say that

5 **Man sollte immer die Wahrheit sagen**
One should always tell the truth
Er wußte nicht, was er tun sollte
He didn't know what to do (*what he should do*)

6 **Ich soll dir helfen**
I am to help you (*I have been told to help you*)
Du sollst sofort deine Frau anrufen
You are to phone your wife at once (*She has left a message asking you to ring*)

7 **Er soll sehr reich sein**
I've heard he's very rich/He is said to be very rich

8 **Es soll niemand sagen, daß die Schotten geizig sind!**
Let no-one say the Scots are mean!
Sie sagte mir, ich solle damit aufhören
She told me to stop it

9 **Das Kind will LKW-Fahrer werden**
The child wants to become a lorry driver

10 **Willst du eins?** Do you want one?
Willst du (möchtest du) etwas trinken?
Do you want (would you like) something to drink?

11 **Er wollte nichts sagen** He refused to say anything

12 **Ich wollte gerade anrufen** I was just about to phone

13 **Keiner will es gewesen sein** No-one admits to doing it

Modal Auxiliary Verbs (contd)

Conjugation and Use

- Modal verbs have unusual present tenses (→**1**)
  Their principal parts are given on pp 86 to 97.

- Each modal verb has two past participles.
  The first, which is the more common, is the same as the infinitive form and is used where the modal is modifying a verb (→**2**)
  The second resembles a normal weak past participle and is used only where no verb is being modified (see the verb list, p 86) (→**3**)

- The verb modified by the modal is placed in its infinitive form at the end of a clause (→**4**)

- Where the modal is used in a compound tense, its past participle in the form of the infinitive is also placed at the end of a clause, immediately after the modified verb (→**5**)

- If the modal verb is modifying a verb, and if the modal is used in a compound tense in a subordinate clause, then the normal word order for subordinate clauses (see p 228) does not apply. The auxiliary used to form the compound tense of the modal is not placed right at the end of the subordinate clause, but instead comes before both infinitives (→**6**)
  Such constructions are usually avoided in German, by using a simple tense in place of a compound. (For notes on the use of tenses in German, see p 58ff) (→**7**)

- A modified verb which expresses motion may be omitted entirely if an adverb or adverbial phrase is present to indicate the movement or destination (→**8**)

1 dürfen
  ich/er/sie/es darf
  du darfst
  wir/sie/Sie dürfen
  ihr dürft

mögen
  ich/er/sie/es mag
  du magst
  wir/sie/Sie mögen
  ihr mögt

sollen
  ich/er/sie/es soll
  du sollst
  wir/sie/Sie sollen
  ihr sollt

können
  ich/er/sie/es kann
  du kannst
  wir/sie/Sie können
  ihr könnt

müssen
  ich/er/sie/es muß
  du mußt
  wir/sie/Sie müssen
  ihr müßt

wollen
  ich/er/sie/es will
  du willst
  wir/sie/Sie wollen
  ihr wollt

2 wollen: Past participle **wollen**
  Er hat kommen wollen he wanted to come
3 wollen: Past participle **gewollt**
  Hast du es gewollt? Did you want it?
4 Er kann gut schwimmen He can swim well
5 Wir haben das Haus nicht kaufen wollen
  We didn't want to buy the house
  Sie wird dich bald sehen wollen
  She will want to see you soon
6 *Compare*:
  Obwohl wir das Haus gekauft haben, ...
  Although we bought the house ...
  Obwohl wir das Haus haben kaufen wollen, ...
  Although we wanted to buy the house ...
7 Obwohl wir das Haus kaufen wollten ...
  Although we wanted to buy the house ...
8 Ich muß nach Hause I must go home
  Die Kinder sollen jetzt ins Bett
  The children have to go to bed now

Use of Tenses

Continuous Forms

- Unlike English, the German verb does not distinguish between its simple and continuous forms (→1)
- To emphasize continuity, the following may be used:
    simple tense plus an adverb or adverbial phrase (→2)
    am or **beim** plus an infinitive used as a noun (→3)
    eben/gerade dabei sein zu plus an infinitive (→4)

The Present

- The present tense is used in German with **seit** or **seitdem** where English uses a past tense to show an action which began in the past and still continues (→5)
    If the action is finished, or does not continue, a past tense is used (→6)
- The present is commonly used with future meaning (→7)

The Future

- The present is often used as a future tense (→7)
- The future tense is used however to:
    emphasize the future (→8)
    express doubt or supposition about the future (→9)
    express future intention (→10)

The Future Perfect

- Used as in English to mean *shall/will have done* (→11)
- It is used in German to express a supposition (→12)
- In conversation it is replaced by the perfect (→13)

The Conditional

- May be used in place of the imperfect subjunctive to express improbable condition (see p 62) (→14)
- Is used in indirect statements or questions to replace the future subjunctive in conversation or where the subjunctive form is not distinctive (→15)

Continued

 1 **ich tue** I do (*simple form*) OR I am doing (*continuous*)
   er rauchte he smoked OR he was smoking
   sie hat gelesen she has read OR she has been reading
   es ist geschickt worden it is sent OR it is being sent
 2 **Er kochte gerade das Abendessen**
   He was cooking the supper
   Nun spricht sie mit ihm Now she's talking to him
 3 **Ich bin am Bügeln** I am ironing
 4 **Wir waren eben dabei, einige Briefe zu schreiben**
   We were just writing a few letters
 5 **Ich wohne seit drei Jahren hier**
   I have been living here for three years
   Seit ich hier wohne, fühle ich mich wohl
   I've been feeling at home since I've lived here
 6 **Seit er krank ist, hat er uns nicht besucht**
   He hasn't visited us since he's been ill
   Seit seiner Verlobung habe ich ihn nicht gesehen
   I haven't seen him since his engagement
 7 **Wir fahren nächstes Jahr nach Griechenland**
   We're going to Greece next year
 8 **Das werde ich erst nächstes Jahr machen können**
   I won't be able to do that until next year
 9 **Wenn er zurückkommt, wird er mir bestimmt helfen**
   He's sure to help me when he returns
10 **Ich werde ihm helfen** I'm going to help him
11 **Bis Sonntag wird er es gelesen haben**
   He will have read it by Sunday
12 **Das wird Herr Keute gewesen sein**
   That must have been Herr Keute
13 **Bis du zurückkommst, haben wir alles aufgeräumt**
   We'll have tidied up by the time you get back
14 **Wenn ich eins hätte, würde ich es dir geben**
   If I had one I would give it to you
   Wenn er jetzt bloß kommen würde!
   If only he would get here!
15 **Er fragte, ob wir fahren würden**
   He asked if we were going to go

Use of Tenses (contd)

The Conditional Perfect
- May be used in place of the pluperfect subjunctive in a sentence containing a **wenn**-clause (→**1**)
- But the pluperfect subjunctive is preferred (→**2**)

The Imperfect
- Is used in German with **seit** or **seitdem** where the pluperfect is used in English to show an action which began in the remote past and continued to a point in the more recent past (→**3**)
  For discontinued actions the pluperfect is used (→**4**)
- Used to describe past actions which have no link with the present as far as the speaker is concerned (→**5**)
  for narrative purposes (→**6**)
  for repeated, habitual or prolonged past action (→**7**)
See also the note on the **Perfect** (below).

The Perfect
- Is used to translate the English perfect tense *I have spoken, he has been reading* (→**8**)
- Describes past actions or events which still have a link with the present or the speaker (→**9**)
- Is used in conversation and similar communication (→**10**)
NOTE: In practice however the perfect and imperfect are often interchangeable in German usage and in spoken German a mixture of both is common.

The Pluperfect
- Is used to translate *had done/had been doing*, except in conjunction with **seit/seitdem** (see **Imperfect**) (→**11**)

The Subjunctive
For uses of the subjunctive tenses, see pp 62 to 67.

1 **Wenn du es gesehen hättest, würdest du's** geglaubt haben
  You would have believed it if you'd seen it
2 **Hättest du es gesehen, so hättest du es** geglaubt
  If you had seen it, you'd have believed it
  Wenn ich das nur nicht gemacht hätte!
  If only I hadn't done it!
  Wäre ich nur da gewesen! If I'd only been there
3 **Sie war seit ihrer Heirat als Lehrerin** beschäftigt
  She had been working as a teacher since her marriage
4 **Ihren Sohn hatten sie seit zwölf Jahren nicht** gesehen
  They hadn't seen their son for twelve years
5 **Er kam zu spät, um teilnehmen zu können**
  He arrived too late to take part
6 **Das Mädchen stand auf, wusch sich das Gesicht, und verließ das Haus**
  The girl got up, washed her face and went out
7 **Wir machten jeden Tag einen kleinen Spaziergang**
  We went (used to go) for a little walk every day
8 **Ich habe ihn heute nicht** gesehen
  I haven't seen him today
9 **Ich habe ihr nichts davon** erzählt
  I didn't tell her anything about it
  Gestern sind wir in die Stadt gefahren und haben uns ein paar Sachen gekauft
  Yesterday we went into town and bought ourselves a few things
10 **Hast du den Krimi gestern abend im Fernsehen** gesehen?
  Did you see the thriller on television last night?
11 **Sie waren schon weggefahren**
  They had already left
  Diese Bücher hatten sie schon gelesen
  They had already read these books

The Subjunctive: when to use it

The subjunctive form in English has almost died out, leaving only a few examples such as:
  if I *were* rich/if only he *were* to come/so *be* it

German however makes much wider use of subjunctive forms, especially in formal, educated or literary contexts. Although there is a growing tendency to use indicatives in spoken German, subjunctives are still very common.

- The indicative tenses in German display fact or certainty. The subjunctives show unreality, uncertainty, speculation about a situation or any doubt in the speaker's mind (→1)
  Subjunctives are also used in indirect speech, as shown on pp 66 and 67.

- For how to form all tenses of the subjunctive, the reader is referred to the relevant sections on Simple Tenses (pp 6 to 17) and Compound Tenses (pp 22 to 29). See also the Subjunctive in Reported Speech (p 66).

- The **imperfect subjunctive** is very common. It is important to note that the imperfect subjunctive form does not always represent actions performed in the past (→2)

Uses of the Subjunctive in German

- To show improbable condition (e.g. if he *came*, he would …)
  The *if*-clause (**wenn** in German) has a verb in the imperfect subjunctive and the main clause can have either an imperfect subjunctive or a conditional (→3)

Continued

1 *INDICATIVE*
Das stimmt
That's true
Es ist eine Unverschämtheit
It's a scandal

SUBJUNCTIVE
Es könnte doch wahr sein
It could well be true
Sie meint, es sei eine Unverschämtheit
She thinks it's a scandal   (*speaker not necessarily in agreement with her*)

2 *imperfect subjunctive expressing the future*
Wenn ich morgen nur da sein könnte!
If only I could be there tomorrow!

expressing the present/immediate future
Wenn er jetzt nur käme!
If only he would come now!

speaker's opinion, referring to present or future
Sie wäre die Beste
She's the best

3 Wenn du kämest, wäre ich froh
OR
Wenn du kämest, würde ich froh sein
I should be happy if you came

Wenn es mir nicht gefiele, würde ich es nicht bezahlen
OR
Wenn es mir nicht gefiele, bezahlte ich es nicht
If I wasn't happy with it, I wouldn't pay for it
(*The second form is less likely, as the imperfect subjunctive and imperfect indicative forms of* **bezahlen** *are identical*)

The Subjunctive: when to use it (contd)

- The imperfect of **sollen** or **wollen**, or a conditional tense might be used in the **wenn**-clause to replace an uncommon imperfect subjunctive, or a subjunctive which is not distinct from the same tense of the indicative (→**1**)

- To show unfulfilled condition (if he *had come*, he would have...)
The **wenn**-clause requires a pluperfect subjunctive, the main clause a pluperfect subjunctive or conditional perfect (→**2**)
NOTE: The indicative is used to express a *probable* condition, as in English (→**3**)
wenn can be omitted from conditional clauses. The verb must then follow the subject and **dann** or **so** usually begins the main clause (→**4**)

- With **selbst wenn** (*even if/even though*) (→**5**)

- With **wenn ... nur** (*if only ...*) (→**6**)

- To speculate or make assumptions (→**7**)

- After **als** (*as if/as though*) (→**8**)

- Where there is uncertainty or doubt (→**9**)

- To make a polite enquiry (→**10**)

- To indicate theoretical possibility or unreality (→**11**)

- As an alternative to the conditional perfect (→**12**)

1 Wenn er mich so sehen würde, würde er mich für verrückt halten!
OR
Wenn er mich so sehen würde, hielte er mich für verrückt!
OR
Wenn er mich so sehen sollte, würde er mich für verrückt halten!
If he saw me like this, he would think I was mad!
(Wenn er mich so sähe *would sound rather stilted*)

2 Wenn du pünktlich gekommen wärest, hättest du ihn gesehen
OR
Wenn du pünktlich gekommen wärest, würdest du ihn gesehen haben
If you had been on time, you would have seen him

3 Wenn ich ihn sehe, gebe ich es ihm
If I see him I'll give him it

4 Hättest du mich nicht gesehen, so wäre ich schon weg
If you hadn't seen me, I would have been gone by now

5 Selbst wenn er etwas wüßte, würde er nichts sagen
Even if he knew about it, he wouldn't say anything

6 Wenn wir nur erfolgreich wären! If only we were successful!

7 Und wenn er recht hätte? What if he were right?
Eine Frau, die das sagen würde (*or* **die das sagte), müßte Feministin sein!**
Any woman who would say that must be a feminist!

8 Er sah aus, als sei er krank
He looked as if he were ill

9 Er wußte nicht, wie es ihr jetzt ginge
He didn't know how she was

10 Wäre da sonst noch etwas? Will there be anything else?

11 Er stellte sich vor, wie gut er in dem Anzug aussähe
He imagined how good he would look in the suit

12 Ich hätte ihn gesehen = Ich würde ihn gesehen haben
I would have seen him

The Subjunctive in Indirect Speech

What a person asks or thinks can be reported in one of two ways,
either **directly**:

Tom said, "I have been on holiday"
    OR **indirectly**:
Tom said (that) he had been on holiday

- In English, indirect, or reported, speech can be indicated by a
  change in tense of what has been reported:
      He said, "*I know* your sister"
      He said (that) *he knew* my sister
  In German the change is not in tense, but from indicative to
  subjunctive (→**1**)

- These are two ways of introducing indirect speech in German,
  similar to the parallel English constructions:
  1. The clause which reports what is said may be introduced by
     daß (*that*). The finite verb or auxiliary comes at the end of
     the clause (→**2**)
  2. **daß** may be omitted. The verb in this case must stand in
     second position in the clause, instead of being placed at the
     end (→**3**)

Forms of the Subjunctive in Indirect Speech

See the conjugation of verbs in the subjunctive (pp 8 to 15 and 26
to 31). In indirect (or reported) speech, wherever the present
subjunctive is identical to the present indicative form, the
imperfect subjunctive is used instead (→**4**)

1 Er sagte: "Sie kennt deine Schwester"
He said, "She knows your sister"
Er sagte, sie kenne meine Schwester
He said she knew my sister
"Habe ich zu viel gesagt?", fragte er
"Did I say too much?", he asked
Er fragte, ob er zuviel gesagt habe
He asked if he had said too much

2 Er hat uns gesagt, daß er Italienisch spreche
He told us that he spoke Italian

3 Er hat uns gesagt, er spreche Italienisch
He told us he spoke Italian

4 *PRESENT SUBJUNCTIVE IN INDIRECT SPEECH*

   WEAK VERBS e.g. **holen** to fetch:

ich holte	**wir holten**
du holest	ihr holet
er hole	**sie holten**

   STRONG VERBS e.g. **singen** to sing:

ich sänge	**wir sängen**
du singest	ihr singet
er singe	**sie sängen**

Verbs with Prefixes

Many verbs in German begin with a prefix. A prefix is a word or part of a word which precedes the verb stem (→**1**)

- Often the addition of a prefix changes the meaning of the basic verb (→**2**)

- Prefixes may be found in strong, weak or mixed verbs. Adding a prefix may occasionally change the verb conjugation (→**3**)

- There are four kinds of prefix and each behaves in a slightly different way, as shown on the following pages. Prefixes may be:

  > inseparable (→**4**)
  >
  > separable (→**5**)
  >
  > double (→**6**)
  >
  > variable, i.e. either separable or inseparable, depending on the verb (→**7**)

Continued

1 zu + geben = zugeben
   an + ziehen = anziehen

2 nehmen to take
   zunehmen to put on weight, to increase
   sich **be**nehmen to behave

3 *WEAK:*   *STRONG:*
   suchen   to look for   stehen   to stand
   versuchen   to try   **ver**stehen   to understand
   besuchen   to visit   **auf**stehen   to get up

   WEAK: *WEAK:*
   löschen   to extinguish   fehlen   to bc missing
   STRONG: *STRONG:*
   erlöschen   to go out   **emp**fehlen   to recommend

4 **ent**decken to discover
   er entdeckt, er entdeckte, er hat entdeckt

5 **mit**machen to join in
   er macht mit, er machte mit, er hat mitgemacht

6 **aus**verkaufen to sell off
   er verkauft aus, er verkaufte aus, er hat ausverkauft

7 **wieder**holen to repeat
   er wiederholt, er wiederholte, er hat wiederholt

   wieder(-)holen to fetch back
   er holt wieder, er holte wieder, er hat wiedergeholt

Verbs with Prefixes (contd)

Inseparable Prefixes

- The eight inseparable prefixes are:

    be-   **emp-**

    ge-   **ent-**

    er-   **miß-**

    ver-   **zer-** (→1)

- These exist only as prefixes, and cannot be words in their own right.

- They are never separated from the verb stem, whatever tense of the verb is used (→2)

- Inseparable prefixes are always unstressed (→3)

- They have no **ge-** in their past participles (see p 50) (→4)

Continued

1 **beschreiben** to describe
   gehören to belong
   erhalten to contain
   verlieren to lose
   empfangen to receive
   enttäuschen to disappoint
   mißtrauen to mistrust
   zerlegen to dismantle

2 **besuchen** to visit:

   Er besucht uns regelmäßig
   He visits us regularly
   Er besuchte uns jeden Tag
   He used to visit us every day
   Er hat uns jeden Tag besucht
   He visited us every day
   Er wird uns morgen besuchen
   He will visit us tomorrow
   Besuche sofort deine Tante!
   Visit your aunt at once

3 erlauben, verstehen, empfangen, vergessen

4 *COMPARE*:
   verstehen: wir haben verstanden we understood
   stehen: wir haben gestanden we stood

   empfangen: wir haben empfangen we received
   fangen: wir haben gefangen we caught

Verbs with Prefixes (contd)

Separable Prefixes

Some common examples are:

ab	empor	herbei	hinauf	nieder
an	entgegen	herein	hinaus	vor
auf	fest	herüber	hindurch	vorbei
aus	frei	herum	hinein	vorüber
bei	her	herunter	hinüber	weg
da(r)	herab	hervor	hinunter	zu
davon	heran	hierher	los	zurecht
dazu	herauf	hin	mit	zurück
ein	heraus	hinab	nach	zusammen

- Unlike inseparable prefixes, separable prefixes may be words in their own right. Indeed, nouns, adjectives, adverbs and even other verbs are often used as separable prefixes (→1)

- The past participle of a verb with a separable prefix is formed with **ge-**. It comes between the verb and the prefix (→2)

- In main clauses, the prefix is placed at the end of the clause if the verb is in a simple tense (i.e. present, imperfect or imperative form) (→3)

- In subordinate clauses, whatever the tense of the verb, the prefix is attached to the verb and the resulting whole placed at the end of the clause (→4)

- Where an infinitive construction requiring **zu** is used (see p 46), the **zu** is placed between the infinitive and prefix to form one word (→5)

1 *noun + verb*: **teilnehmen** to take part
verb + verb: **kennenlernen** to get to know
adjective + verb: **loswerden** to get free of
adverb + verb: **niederlegen** to lay down

2 **Er ist gestern spazierengegangen**
He went for a walk yesterday
Wir sind an der Grenze zurückgewiesen worden
We were turned back at the border

3 **wegbringen**: to take for repair, to take away
PRESENT: **Wir bringen das Auto weg**
IMPERFECT: **Wir brachten das Auto weg**
IMPERATIVE: **Bringt das Auto weg!**

CONDITIONAL: **Wir würden das Auto wegbringen**
FUTURE: **Wir werden das Auto wegbringen**
PERFECT: **Wir haben das Auto weggebracht**
PERFECT PASSIVE: **Das Auto ist weggebracht worden**
PLUPERFECT SUBJUNCTIVE: **Wir hätten das Auto weggebracht**

4 *PRESENT*: **Weil wir das Auto wegbringen, ...**
IMPERFECT: **Daß wir das Auto wegbrachten, ...**
PERFECT: **Nachdem wir das Auto weggebracht haben, ...**
PLUPERFECT SUBJUNCTIVE: **Wenn wir das Auto weggebracht hätten, ...**
FUTURE: **Obwohl wir das Auto wegbringen werden, ...**

5 **Um das Auto rechtzeitig wegzubringen, müssen wir morgen früh aufstehen**
In order to take the car in on time, we shall have to get up early tomorrow

Verbs with Prefixes (contd)

Variable Prefixes

These are:
über	**um**
unter	**voll**
durch	**wider**
hinter	**wieder**

- These can be separable or inseparable (→**1**)

- Often they are used separably and inseparably with the same verb. In such cases the verb and prefix will tend to retain their basic meanings if the prefix is used separably, but adopt figurative meanings when the prefix is used inseparably (→**2**)

- Variable prefixes behave as separable prefixes when used separably, and as inseparable prefixes when used inseparably (→**3**)

Double Prefixes

These occur where a verb with an inseparable prefix is preceded by a separable prefix (→**4**)

- The separable prefix behaves as described on p 72, the verb plus inseparable prefix representing the basic verb to which the separable prefix is attached (→**5**)

- Unlike other separable verbs, however, verbs with double prefixes have no **ge-** in their past participles (→**6**)

1 unternehmen (*inseparable*) to undertake, take on:

Wir haben in den Ferien vieles unternommen
We did a great deal in the holidays
Du unternimmst zuviel
You take on too much

untergehen (*separable*) to sink, go down:

Die Sonne ist untergegangen
The sun has gone down/has set
Die Sonne geht unter
The sun is going down/is setting

2 etwas wiederholen (*separable*) to retrieve something
etwas wiederholen (*inseparable*) to repeat something

3 Er holte ihr die Tasche wieder
He brought her back her bag
Er wiederholte den Satz
He repeated the sentence

4 ausverkaufen to sell off

5 Er verkauft alles aus
He's selling everything off
Um alles auszuverkaufen ...
In order to sell everything off ...
Er wird alles ausverkaufen
He'll be selling everything off

6 Aber er hat doch alles ausverkauft
But he's sold everything off

Verbs followed by Prepositions

- Some verbs in English usage require a preposition (*for/with/by* etc) for their completion.
  This also happens in German, though the prepositions used with German verbs may not be those expected from their English counterparts (→**1**)

- The preposition used may significantly alter the meaning of a verb in German (→**2**)

- Occasionally German verbs use a preposition where their English equivalents do not (→**3**)

- Prepositions used with verbs behave as normal prepositions and affect the *case* of the following noun (see p 198).

- A verb plus preposition may be followed by a clause containing another verb rather than by a noun or pronoun. This often corresponds to an *-ing* construction in English:
  Thank you for *coming*
  In German, this is dealt with in two ways:
  1. Where the "verb-plus-preposition" construction has the same subject as the following verb, the preposition is preceded by **da-** or **dar-** and the following verb becomes an infinitive used with **zu** (→**4**)
  2. Where the subject of the "verb-plus-preposition" is not the same as for the following verb, a **daß** clause is used (→**5**)

- Following clauses may also be introduced by interrogatives (**ob, wie** etc) if the meaning demands them (→**6**)

Continued

1   Compare:

    GERMAN   *ENGLISH*
    sich sehnen **nach**   to long *for*
    warten **auf**   to wait *for*
    bitten **um**   to ask *for*

2   **bestehen** to pass (an examination/a test *etc*)
    bestehen aus to consist of
    bestehen auf to insist on

    sich freuen auf to look forward to
    sich freuen über to be pleased about

3   **diskutieren über** to discuss

4   **Ich freue mich sehr darauf, mal wieder mit ihm zu arbeiten**
    I am looking forward to working with him again

5   **Ich freue mich sehr darauf, daß du morgen kommst**
    I am looking forward to your coming tomorrow
    Er sorgte dafür, daß die Kinder immer gut gepflegt waren
    He saw to it that the children were always well cared for

6   **Er dachte lange darüber nach, ob er es wirklich kaufen wollte**
    He thought for ages about whether he really wanted to buy it
    Sie freut sich darüber, wie schnell ihre Schüler gelernt haben
    She is pleased at how quickly her students have learned

Verbs followed by Prepositions (contd)

Common verbs followed by preposition + accusative case:
achten auf to pay attention to, keep an eye on (→**1**)
sich amüsieren über to laugh at, smile about
sich ärgern über to get annoyed about/with
sich bewerben um to apply for (→**2**)
bitten um to ask for (→**3**)
denken an to be thinking of (→**4**)
denken über to hold an opinion of, think about (→**5**)
sich erinnern an to remember
sich freuen auf to look forward to
sich freuen über to be pleased about (→**6**)
sich gewöhnen an to get used to (→**7**)
sich interessieren für to be interested in (→**8**)
kämpfen um to fight for
sich kümmern um to take care of, see to
nachdenken über to ponder, reflect on (→**9**)
sich unterhalten über to talk about
sich verlassen auf to rely on, depend on (→**10**)
warten auf to wait for

Common verbs followed by preposition + dative case:
abhängen von to be dependent on (→**11**)
sich beschäftigen mit to occupy oneself with (→**12**)
bestehen aus to consist of (→**13**)
leiden an/unter to suffer from (→**14**)
neigen zu to be inclined to
riechen nach to smell of (→**15**)
schmecken nach to taste of
sich sehnen nach to long for
sterben an to die of
teilnehmen an to take part in (→**16**)
träumen von to dream of (→**17**).
sich verabschieden von to say goodbye to
sich verstehen mit to get along with, get on with
zittern vor to tremble with (→**18**)

1 **Er mußte auf die Kinder achten**
   He had to keep an eye on the children
2 **Sie hat sich um die Stelle als Sekretärin beworben**
   She applied for the post of secretary
3 **Die Kinder baten ihre Mutter um Plätzchen**
   The children asked their mother for some biscuits
4 **Woran denkst du?** What are you thinking about?
   Daran habe ich gar nicht mehr gedacht
   I'd forgotten about that
5 **Wie denkt ihr darüber?** What do you think about it?
6 **Ich freute mich sehr darüber, Johannes besucht zu haben**
   I was very glad I had visited Johannes
7 **Man gewöhnt sich an alles** One gets used to anything
8 **Sie interessiert sich sehr für Politik**
   She is very interested in politics
9 **Er hatte schon lange darüber nachgedacht**
   He had been thinking about it for a long time
10 **Er verläßt sich darauf, daß seine Frau alles tut**
   He relies on his wife to do everything
11 **Das hängt davon ab** It all depends
12 **Sie sind im Moment sehr damit beschäftigt, ihr neues Haus
   in Ordnung zu bringen**
   They are very busy sorting out their new house at the moment
13 **Dieser Kuchen besteht aus Eiern, Mehl und Zucker**
   This cake consists of eggs, flour and sugar
14 **Sie hat lange an dieser Krankheit gelitten**
   She suffered from this illness for a long time
   Alte Leute können sehr unter der Einsamkeit leiden
   Old people can suffer dreadful loneliness
15 **Der Kuchen roch nach Zimt**
   The cake smelled of cinnamon
16 **Sie hat an der Bonner Tagung teilnehmen müssen**
   She had to attend the Bonn conference
17 **Er hat von seinem Urlaub geträumt**
   He dreamt of his holiday
18 **Er zitterte vor Freude** He was trembling with joy

Verbs followed by the Dative

Some verbs have a direct object and an indirect object. In the English sentence *He gave me a book, me* (= *to me*) is the indirect object and would appear in the dative case in German; *a book* is the direct object of *gave* and would be in the accusative (→**1**)

- In German, as in English, this type of verb is usually concerned with giving or telling something to someone, or with performing an action for someone (→**2**)

- The normal word order after such verbs is for the direct object to follow the indirect, *except* where the direct object is a personal pronoun (see p 224) (→**2**)
  This order may be reversed for emphasis (→**3**)

- Some examples of verbs followed by the dative in this way:

anbieten	**bringen**	**beweisen**
erzählen	**geben**	**gönnen**
kaufen	**leihen**	**mitteilen**
schenken	**schicken**	**schreiben**
schulden	**verkaufen**	**zeigen** (→**4**)

- Certain verbs in German however can be followed *only* by an indirect object in the dative case. These should be noted especially, since most of them are quite different from their English equivalents:

begegnen	**danken**	**fehlen**
gefallen	**gehören**	**gelingen**
gleichen	**gratulieren**	**helfen**
imponieren	**mißtrauen**	**nachgehen**
schaden	**schmecken**	**schmeicheln**
trauen	**trotzen**	**vorangehen**
weh tun	**widersprechen**	**widerstehen** (→**5**)

- For how to form the passive of such verbs, see p 36.

1 Er gab mir ein Buch He gave me a book

2 Er wusch dem Kind (*indirect*) **das Gesicht** (*direct*)
He washed the child's face
Er erzählte ihm (*indirect*) **eine Geschichte** (*direct*)
He told him a story
BUT
Er hat sie (*direct*) **meiner Mutter** (*indirect*) **gezeigt**
He showed it to my mother
Kaufst du es (*direct*) **mir** (*indirect*)?
Will you buy it for me?

3 Er wollte das Buch (*direct*) **seiner Mutter** (*indirect*) **geben**
(*This emphasises* **seiner Mutter**)
He wanted to give the book to his mother

4 Er bot ihr die Arbeitsstelle an He offered her the job
Bringst du mir eins? Will you bring me one?
Ich gönne dir das neue Kleid
I want you to have the new dress
Er hat ihr mitgeteilt, daß ... He told her that ...
Ich schenke meiner Mutter Parfüm zum Geburtstag
I am giving my mother perfume for her birthday
Das schulde ich ihm I owe him that
Zeig es mir! Show me it!

5 Er ist seinem Freund in der Stadt begegnet
He bumped into his friend in town
Mir fehlt der Mut dazu I don't have the courage
Es ist ihnen gelungen They succeeded
Wem gehört dieses Buch? Whose book is this?
Er wollte ihr nicht helfen He refused to help her
Ich gratuliere dir! Congratulations!
Rauchen schadet der Gesundheit
Smoking is bad for your health
Das Essen hat ihnen gut geschmeckt
They enjoyed the meal

There is/There are

There are three ways of expressing this in German:

es gibt

- This is always used in the singular form, and is followed by an accusative object which may be either singular or plural (→**1**)
- **es gibt** is used to refer to things of a general nature or location (→**2**)
- It also has some idiomatic usages (→**3**)

es ist/es sind

- The **es** here merely introduces the real subject. The verb therefore becomes plural where the real subject is plural. The real subject is in the nominative case (→**4**)
- The **es** is not required and is therefore omitted when the verb and real subject come together. This happens when inversion of subject and verb occurs (see p 226) and in subordinate clauses (→**5**)
- **es ist** or **es sind** are used to refer to
  1. subjects with a specific and confined location.
     This location must always be mentioned either by name or by **da, darauf, darin** etc (→**6**)
  2. temporary existence (→**7**)
  3. as a beginning to a story (→**8**)

The Passive Voice

Often *there is/there are* in English will be rendered by a verb in the passive voice in German (→**9**)

1 **Es gibt zu viele Probleme dabei**
   There are too many problems involved
   Es gibt kein besseres Bier There's no better beer

2 **Es gibt bestimmt Regen**
   It's definitely going to rain
   Ruhe hat es bei uns nie gegeben
   There has never been any peace here

3 **Was gibt's (= gibt es) zum Essen?** What's there to eat?
   Was gibt's? What's wrong? What's up?
   So was gibt's doch nicht! That's impossible!

4 **Es waren zwei ältere Leute unten im Hof**
   There were two elderly people down in the yard
   Es sind so viele Touristen da
   There are so many tourists there

5 **Unten im Hof waren zwei ältere Leute**
   Down in the yard were two elderly people
   Wenn so viele Touristen da sind ...
   If there are so many tourists there ...

6 **Es waren viele Flaschen Sekt im Keller**
   There were a lot of bottles of champagne in the cellar
   Ein Brief lag auf dem Tisch. Es waren auch zwei Bücher darauf
   A letter lay on the table. There were also two books on it

7 **Es war niemand da** There was no-one there

8 **Es war einmal ein König ...**
   Once upon a time there was a king ...

9 **Es wurde auf der Party viel getrunken**
   There was a lot of drinking at the party

Use of "es" as an anticipatory object

Many verbs can have as their object a **daß** clause or an infinitive
with **zu** (→**1**)

- With some verbs **es** is used as an object to anticipate this clause
  or infinitive phrase (→**2**)
- When the clause or infinitive phrase begins the sentence, **es** is
  not used in the main clause but its place may be taken by an
  optional **das** (→**3**)

Common verbs which usually have the "es" object

> **es ablehnen, zu** to refuse to
> **es aushalten, zu tun/daß** to stand doing (→**4**)
> **es ertragen, zu tun/daß** to endure doing
> **es leicht haben, zu** to find it easy to (→**5**)
> **es nötig haben, zu** to need to (→**6**)
> **es satt haben, zu** to have had enough of (doing)
> **es verstehen, zu** to know how to (→**7**)

Common verbs which often have the "es" object

> **es jemandem anhören/ansehen, daß** to tell by listening to/
> looking at someone that (→**8**)
> **es begreifen, daß/warum/wie** to understand that/why/how
> **es bereuen, zu tun/daß** to regret having done/that
> **es leugnen, daß** to deny that (→**9**)
> **es unternehmen, zu** to undertake to
> **es jemandem verbieten, zu** to forbid someone to
> **es jemandem vergeben, daß** to forgive someone for (doing)
> **es jemandem verschweigen, daß** not to tell someone that
> **es jemandem verzeihen, daß** to forgive someone for (doing)
> **es wagen zu** to dare to

1 **Er wußte, daß wir pünktlich kommen würden**
He knew that we would come on time
Sie fing an zu lachen
She began to laugh

2 **Er hatte es abgelehnt mitzufahren**
He had refused to come

3 **Daß es Wolfgang war, das haben wir ihr verschwiegen**
OR: **Daß es Wolfgang war, haben wir ihr verschwiegen**
We didn't tell her that it was Wolfgang

4 **Ich halte es nicht mehr aus, bei ihnen zu arbeiten**
I can't stand working for them any longer

5 **Er hatte es nicht leicht, sie zu überreden**
He didn't have an easy job persuading them

6 **Ich habe es nicht nötig, mit dir darüber zu reden**
I don't have to talk to you about it

7 **Er versteht es, Autos zu reparieren**
He knows about repairing cars

8 **Man hörte es ihm sofort an, daß er kein Deutscher war**
OR: **Daß er kein Deutscher war, (das) hörte man ihm sofort an**
One could tell immediately (from the way he spoke) that he wasn't German

 Man sieht es ihm sofort an, daß er dein Bruder ist
OR: **Daß er dein Bruder ist, (das) sieht man ihm sofort an**
One can tell at a glance that he's your brother

9 **Er hat es nie geleugnet, das Geld genommen zu haben**
He has never denied taking the money

Strong and Mixed Verbs - Principal Parts

INFINITIVE		3RD PERSON PRESENT
backen	to bake	**er bäckt**
befehlen	to command	**er befiehlt**
beginnen	to begin	**er beginnt**
beißen	to bite	**er beißt**
bergen	to rescue	**er birgt**
bersten	to burst *intr*	**er birst**
betrügen	to deceive	**er betrügt**
biegen	to bend *tr*/to turn *intr*	**er biegt**
bieten	to offer	**er bietet**
binden	to tie	**er bindet**
bitten	to ask for	**er bittet**
blasen	to blow	**er bläst**
bleiben	to remain	**er bleibt**
braten	to fry	**er brät**
brechen	to break	**er bricht**
brennen	to burn	**er brennt**
bringen	to bring	**er bringt**
denken	to think	**er denkt**
dreschen	to thresh	**er drischt**
dringen	to penetrate	**er dringt**
dürfen	to be allowed to	**er darf**
empfehlen	to recommend	**er empfiehlt**
erlöschen	to go out (*fire, light*)	**er erlischt**
erschallen	to resound	**er erschallt**
erschrecken	to be startled[1]	**er erschrickt**
erwägen	to weigh up	**er erwägt**
essen	to eat	**er ißt**
fahren	to travel	**er fährt**

1. **erschrecken** meaning "to frighten" is **weak**:
    erschrecken, erschreckt, erschreckte, hat erschreckt

3RD PERSON IMPERFECT	PERFECT	IMPERFECT SUBJUNCTIVE
er backte	er hat gebacken	er backte
er befahl	er hat befohlen	er befähle
er begann	er hat begonnen	er begänne
er biß	er hat gebissen	er bisse
er barg	er hat geborgen	er bärge
er barst	er ist geborsten	er bärste
er betrog	er hat betrogen	er betröge
er bog	er hat/ist gebogen	er böge
er bot	er hat geboten	er böte
er band	er hat gebunden	er bände
er bat	er hat gebeten	er bäte
er blies	er hat geblasen	er bliese
er blieb	er ist geblieben	er bliebe
er briet	er hat gebraten	er briete
er brach	er hat/ist gebrochen	er bräche
er brannte	er hat gebrannt	er brennte
er brachte	er hat gebracht	er brächte
er dachte	er hat gedacht	er dächte
er drosch	er hat gedroschen	er drösche
er drang	er ist gedrungen	er drange
er durfte	er hat gedurft/dürfen[1]	er dürfte
er empfahl	er hat empfohlen	er empfähle
er erlosch	er ist erloschen	er erlösche
er erschallte	er ist erschollen	er erschölle
er erschrak	er ist erschrocken	er erschräke
er erwog	er hat erwogen	er erwöge
er aß	er hat gegessen	er äße
er fuhr	er ist gefahren	er führe

1. The second (infinitive) form is used when combined with an infinitive construction (see p 56).

Continued

INFINITIVE		3RD PERSON PRESENT
fallen	to fall	**er fällt**
fangen	to catch	**er fängt**
fechten	to fight	**er ficht**
finden	to find	**er findet**
fliegen	to fly	**er fliegt**
fliehen	to flee *tr/intr*	**er flieht**
fließen	to flow	**er fließt**
fressen	to eat (*of animals*)	**er frißt**
frieren	to be cold; freeze over	**er friert**
gebären	to give birth to	**sie gebärt**
geben	to give	**er gibt**
gedeihen	to thrive	**er gedeiht**
gehen	to go	**er geht**
gelingen	to succeed	**es gelingt**
gelten	to be valid	**er gilt**
genesen	to get well	**er genest**
genießen	to enjoy	**er genießt**
geraten	to get into (*a state etc*)	**er gerät**
geschehen	to happen	**es geschieht**
gewinnen	to win	**er gewinnt**
gießen	to pour	**er gießt**
gleichen	to resemble; equal	**er gleicht**
gleiten	to glide	**er gleitet**
glimmen	to glimmer	**er glimmt**
graben	to dig	**er gräbt**
greifen	to grip	**er greift**
haben	to have	**er hat**
halten	to hold, stop	**er hält**
hängen	to hang *intr*[1]	**er hängt**
heben	to lift	**er hebt**
heißen	to be called	**er heißt**

1. **hängen** is **weak** when used transitively.

3RD PERSON IMPERFECT	PERFECT	IMPERFECT SUBJUNCTIVE
er fiel	er ist gefallen	er fiele
er fing	er hat gefangen	er finge
er focht	er hat gefochten	er föchte
er fand	er hat gefunden	er fände
er flog	er hat/ist geflogen	er flöge
er floh	er hat/ist geflohen	er flöhe
er floß	er ist geflossen	er flösse
er fraß	er hat gefressen	er fräße
er fror	er hat/ist gefroren	er fröre
sie gebar	sie hat geboren	sie gebäre
er gab	er hat gegeben	er gäbe
er gedieh	er ist gediehen	er gediehe
er ging	er ist gegangen	er ginge
es gelang	es ist gelungen	es gelänge
er galt	er hat gegolten	er gälte
er genas	er ist genesen	er genäse
er genoß	er hat genossen	er genösse
er geriet	er ist geraten	er geriete
es geschah	es ist geschehen	es geschähe
er gewann	er ist gewonnen	er gewönne
er goß	er hat gegossen	er gösse
er glich	er hat geglichen	er gliche
er glitt	er ist geglitten	er glitte
er glomm	er hat geglommen	er glömme
er grub	er hat gegraben	er grübe
er griff	er hat gegriffen	er griffe
er hatte	er hat gehabt	er hätte
er hielt	er hat gehalten	er hielte
er hing	er hat gehangen	er hinge
er hob	er hat gehoben	er höbe
er hieß	er hat geheißen	er hieße

Continued

INFINITIVE		3RD PERSON PRESENT
helfen	to help	**er hilft**
kennen	to know (*someone etc*)	**er kennt**
klingen	to sound	**er klingt**
kommen	to come	**er kommt**
kneifen	to pinch	**er kneift**
können	to be able to	**er kann**
kriechen	to crawl	**er kriecht**
laden	to load	**er lädt**
lassen	to allow	**er läßt**
laufen	to walk; run	**er läuft**
leiden	to suffer	**er leidet**
leihen	to lend	**er leiht**
lesen	to read	**er liest**
liegen	to lie	**er liegt**
lügen	to tell a lie	**er lügt**
mahlen	to grind	**er mahlt**
messen	to measure	**er mißt**
mißlingen	to fail	**es mißlingt**
mögen	to like to	**er mag**
müssen	to have to	**er muß**
nehmen	to take	**er nimmt**
nennen	to call	**er nennt**
pfeifen	to whistle	**er pfeift**
preisen	to praise	**er preist**
quellen	to gush	**er quillt**
raten	to advise; guess	**er rät**
reiben	to rub	**er reibt**
reißen	to tear *tr/intr*	**er reißt**
reiten	to ride *tr/intr*	**er reitet**

3RD PERSON IMPERFECT	PERFECT	IMPERFECT SUBJUNCTIVE
er half	er hat geholfen	er hülfe
er kannte	er hat gekannt	er kennte
er klang	er hat geklungen	er klänge
er kam	er ist gekommen	er käme
er kniff	er hat gekniffen	er kniffe
er konnte	er hat gekonnt/können[1]	er könnte
er kroch	er ist gekrochen	er kröche
er lud	er hat geladen	er lüde
er ließ	er hat gelassen	er ließe
er lief	er ist gelaufen	er liefe
er litt	er hat gelitten	er litte
er lieh	er hat geliehen	er liehe
er las	er hat gelesen	er läse
er lag	er hat gelegen	er läge
er log	er hat gelogen	er löge
er mahlte	er hat gemahlen	er mahlte
er maß	er hat gemessen	er mäße
es mißlang	es ist mißlungen	es mißlänge
er mochte	er hat gemocht/mögen[1]	er möchte
er mußte	er hat gemußt/müssen[1]	er müßte
er nahm	er hat genommen	er nähme
er nannte	er hat genannt	er nennte
er pfiff	er hat gepfiffen	er pfiffe
er pries	er hat gepriesen	er priese
er quoll	er ist gequollen	er quölle
er riet	er hat geraten	er riete
er rieb	er hat gerieben	er riebe
er riß	er hat/ist gerissen	er risse
er ritt	er hat/ist geritten	er ritte

1. The second (infinitive) form is used when combined with an infinitive construction (see p 56).

Continued

INFINITIVE		3RD PERSON PRESENT
rennen	to run	**er rennt**
riechen	to smell	**er riecht**
ringen	to wrestle	**er ringt**
rinnen	to flow	**er rinnt**
rufen	to shout	**er ruft**
salzen	to salt	**er salzt**
saufen	to booze; drink	**er säuft**
saugen	to suck	**er saugt**
schaffen	to create[1]	**er schafft**
scheiden	to separate *tr/intr*	**er scheidet**
scheinen	to seem; shine	**er scheint**
schelten	to scold	**er schilt**
scheren	to shear	**er schert**
schieben	to shove	**er schiebt**
schießen	to shoot	**er schießt**
schlafen	to sleep	**er schläft**
schlagen	to hit	**er schlägt**
schleichen	to creep	**er schleicht**
schleifen	to grind	**er schleift**
schließen	to close	**er schließt**
schlingen	to wind	**er schlingt**
schmeißen	to fling	**er schmeißt**
schmelzen	to melt *tr/intr*	**er schmilzt**
schneiden	to cut	**er schneidet**
schreiben	to write	**er schreibt**
schreien	to shout	**er schreit**
schreiten	to stride	**er schreitet**
schweigen	to be silent	**er schweigt**

1. **schaffen** meaning "to work hard/manage" is **weak**:
    schaffen, schafft, schaffte, hat geschafft

3RD PERSON IMPERFECT	PERFECT	IMPERFECT SUBJUNCTIVE
er rannte	er ist gerannt	er rennte
er roch	er hat gerochen	er röche
er rang	er hat gerungen	er ränge
er rann	er ist geronnen	er ränne
er rief	er hat gerufen	er riefe
er salzte	er hat gesalzen	er salzte
er soff	er hat gesoffen	er söffe
er sog	er hat gesogen	er söge
er schuf	er hat geschaffen	er schüfe
er schied	er hat/ist geschieden	er schiede
er schien	er hat geschienen	er schiene
er schalt	er hat gescholten	er schölte
er schor	er hat geschoren	er schöre
er schob	er hat geschoben	er schöbe
er schoß	er hat geschossen	er schösse
er schlief	er hat geschlafen	er schliefe
er schlug	er hat geschlagen	er schlüge
er schlich	er ist geschlichen	er schliche
er schliff	er hat geschliffen	er schliffe
er schloß	er hat geschlossen	er schlösse
er schlang	er hat geschlungen	er schlänge
er schmiß	er hat geschmissen	er schmisse
er schmolz	er hat/ist geschmolzen	er schmölze
er schnitt	er hat geschnitten	er schnitte
er schrieb	er hat geschrieben	er schriebe
er schrie	er hat geschrie(e)n	er schriee
er schritt	er ist geschritten	er schritte
er schwieg	er hat geschwiegen	er schwiege

Continued

INFINITIVE		*3RD PERSON PRESENT*
schwellen	to swell *intr*[1]	**er schwillt**
schwimmen	to swim	**er schwimmt**
schwingen	to swing	**er schwingt**
schwören	to vow	**er schwört**
sehen	to see	**er sieht**
sein	to be	**er ist**
senden	to send[2]	**er sendet**
singen	to sing	**er singt**
sinken	to sink	**er sinkt**
sinnen	to ponder	**er sinnt**
sitzen	to sit	**er sitzt**
sollen	to be supposed to be	**er soll**
spalten	to split *tr/intr*	**er spaltet**
speien	to spew	**er speit**
spinnen	to spin	**er spinnt**
sprechen	to speak	**er spricht**
sprießen	to sprout	**er sprießt**
springen	to jump	**er springt**
stechen	to sting/prick	**er sticht**
stehen	to stand	**er steht**
stehlen	to steal	**er stiehlt**
steigen	to climb	**er steigt**
sterben	to die	**er stirbt**
stinken	to stink	**er stinkt**
stoßen	to knock/come across	**er stößt**
streichen	to stroke/wander	**er streicht**
streiten	to quarrel	**er streitet**

1. **schwellen** is **weak** when used transitively:
   schwellen, schwellt, schwellte, hat geschwellt
2. **senden** meaning "to broadcast" is **weak**:
   senden, sendet, sendete, hat gesendet

3RD PERSON IMPERFECT	PERFECT	IMPERFECT SUBJUNCTIVE
er schwoll	er ist geschwollen	er schwölle
er schwamm	er ist geschwommen	er schwömme
er schwang	er hat geschwungen	er schwänge
er schwor	er hat geschworen	er schwüre
er sah	er hat gesehen	er sähe
er war	er ist gewesen	er wäre
er sandte	er hat gesandt	er sendete
er sang	er hat gesungen	er sänge
er sank	er ist gesunken	er sänke
er sann	er hat gesonnen	er sänne
er saß	er hat gesessen	er säße
er sollte	er hat gesollt/sollen[1]	er sollte
er spaltete	er hat/ist gespalten	er spaltete
er spie	er hat gespie(e)n	er spiee
er spann	er hat gesponnen	er spönne
er sprach	er hat gesprochen	er spräche
er sproß	er ist gesprossen	er sprösse
er sprang	er ist gesprungen	er spränge
er stach	er hat gestochen	er stäche
er stand	er hat gestanden	er stünde
er stahl	er hat gestohlen	er stähle
er stieg	er ist gestiegen	er stiege
er starb	er ist gestorben	er stürbe
er stank	er hat gestunken	er stänke
er stieß	er hat/ist gestoßen	er stieße
er strich	er hat/ist gestrichen	er striche
er stritt	er hat gestritten	er stritte

1. The second (infinitive) form is used when combined with an infinitive construction (see p 56).

Continued

INFINITIVE		3RD PERSON PRESENT
tragen	to carry; wear	**er trägt**
treffen	to meet	**er trifft**
treiben	to drive; engage in	**er treibt**
treten	to kick/step	**er tritt**
trinken	to drink	**er trinkt**
tun	to do	**er tut**
verderben	to spoil/go bad	**er verdirbt**
verdrießen	to irritate	**er verdrießt**
vergessen	to forget	**er vergißt**
verlieren	to lose	**er verliert**
vermeiden	to avoid	**er vermeidet**
verschwinden	to disappear	**er verschwindet**
verzeihen	to pardon	**er verzeiht**
wachsen	to grow	**er wächst**
waschen	to wash	**er wäscht**
weichen	to yield	**er weicht**
weisen	to point	**er weist**
wenden	to turn	**er wendet**
werben	to recruit	**er wirbt**
werden	to become	**er wird**
werfen	to throw	**er wirft**
wiegen	to weigh[1]	**er wiegt**
winden	to wind	**er windet**
wissen	to know	**er weiß**
wollen	to want to	**er will**
ziehen	to pull	**er zieht**
zwingen	to force	**er zwingt**

1. **wiegen** meaning "to rock" is **weak**

3RD PERSON IMPERFECT	PERFECT	IMPERFECT SUBJUNCTIVE
er trug	er hat getragen	er trüge
er traf	er hat getroffen	er träfe
er trieb	er hat getrieben	er triebe
er trat	er hat/ist getreten	er träte
er trank	er hat getrunken	er tränke
er tat	er hat getan	er täte
er verdarb	er hat/ist verdorben	er verdürbe
er verdroß	er hat verdrossen	er verdrösse
er vergaß	er hat vergessen	er vergäße
er verlor	er hat verloren	er verlöre
er vermied	er hat vermieden	er vermiede
er verschwand	er ist verschwunden	er verschwände
er verzieh	er hat verziehen	er verziehe
er wuchs	er ist gewachsen	er wüchse
er wusch	er hat gewaschen	er wüsche
er wich	er ist gewichen	er wiche
er wies	er hat gewiesen	er wiese
er wandte	er hat gewandt	er wendete
er warb	er hat geworben	er würbe
er wurde	er ist geworden	er würde
er warf	er hat geworfen	er würfe
er wog	er hat gewogen	er wöge
er wand	er hat gewunden	er wände
er wußte	er hat gewußt	er wüßte
er wollte	er hat gewollt/wollen[1]	er wollte
er zog	er hat gezogen	er zöge
er zwang	er hat gezwungen	er zwänge

1. The second (infinitive) form is used when combined with an infinitive construction (see p 56).

The Declension of Nouns

In German, all nouns may be declined. This means that they may change their form according to their

gender (i.e. masculine, feminine or neuter) (→**1**)

case (i.e. their function in the sentence) (→**2**)

number (i.e. singular or plural) (→**3**)

- Nearly all *feminine* nouns change in the *plural* form by adding **-n** or **-en**. Many *masculine* and *neuter* nouns also change (→**4**)

- *Masculine* and *neuter* nouns, with a few exceptions, add **-s** (**-s** or **-es** for nouns of one syllable) in the *genitive singular* (but see p 110) (→**5**)

- All nouns end in **-n** or **-en** in the *dative plural*. This is added to the nominative plural form, where this does not already end in **-n** (→**6**)

- A good dictionary will provide guidance on how to decline a noun:
  The nominative singular form is given in full, followed by the gender of the noun, then the genitive singular and nominative plural endings are shown where appropriate (→**7**)

- Adjectives used as nouns are declined as adjectives rather than nouns. Their declension endings are therefore dictated by the preceding article, as well as by number, case and gender (see p 140) (→**8**)

Continued

1 der Tisch (*masculine*) the table
die Gabel (*feminine*) the fork
das Mädchen (*neuter*) the girl

2 des Tisches of the table
auf den Tischen on the tables

3 die Tische the tables
die Gabeln the forks
die Mädchen the girls

4

	NOM SING	*NOM PLURAL*
MASC	**der Apfel**	**die Äpfel**
FEM	**die Schule**	**die Schulen**
NEUT	**das Kind**	**die Kinder**

5

	NOM SING	*GEN SING*
MASC	**der Apfel**	**des Apfels**
FEM	**die Schule**	**der Schule**
NEUT	**das Kind**	**des Kind(e)s**

6 den Äpfeln
den Schulen
den Kindern

7 Tiger *m* **-s, -**

NOM SING	**der Tiger**	the tiger
GEN SING	**des Tigers**	of the tiger, the tiger's
NOM PL	**die Tiger**	the tigers

8 der Angestellte   the employee
ein Angestellter   an employee
(die) Angestellten   (the) employees

The Gender of Nouns

In German a noun may be masculine, feminine or neuter. Gender is relatively unpredictable and has to be learned for each noun. This is best done by learning each noun with its definite article, i.e.

der Teppich, die Zeit, das Bild

The following are intended therefore only as guidelines in helping decide the gender of a word.

- Nouns denoting male people and animals are masculine (→**1**)

- Nouns denoting the female of the species, as shown on p 104 are of course feminine (→**2**)

- But nouns denoting an entire species can be of any gender (→**3**)

- Makes of cars identify with **der Wagen** and so are usually masculine (→**4**)

- Makes of aeroplane usually identify with **die Maschine** and so are feminine (→**5**)

- Seasons, months, days of the week, weather features and north, south, east, and west are masculine (→**6**)

- Names of objects that perform an action are usually masculine (→**7**)

- Foreign nouns ending in **-ant, -ast, -ismus, -or** are masculine (→**8**) (But see the list of exceptions below)

- Nouns ending in **-ich, -ig, -ing, -ling** are masculine (→**9**)

Continued

1 der **Hörer** (male) listener
  der **Löwe** (male) lion
  der **Onkel** uncle
  der **Vetter** (male) cousin

2 die **Hörerin** (female) listener
  die **Löwin** lioness
  die **Tante** aunt
  die **Kusine** (female) cousin

3 der **Hund** dog
  die **Schlange** snake
  das **Vieh** cattle

4 der **Mercedes** Mercedes
  der **VW** Volkswagen

5 die **Boeing** Boeing
  die **Concorde** Concorde

6 der **Sommer** summer
  der **Winter** winter
  der **August** August
  der **Freitag** Friday
  der **Wind** wind
  der **Schnee** snow
  der **Norden** north
  der **Osten** east

7 der **Wecker** alarm clock
  der **Computer** computer

8 der **Ballast** ballast
  der **Chauvinismus** chauvinism

9 der **Essig** vinegar
  der **Schmetterling** butterfly

The Gender of Nouns (contd)

- Cardinal numbers are mostly feminine, but fractions are neuter (→**1**)

- Most nouns ending in **-e** are feminine (→**2**)
  EXCEPTIONS :   male people or animals are masculine (→**3**)
  nouns beginning with **Ge-** are normally neuter (*see below*)

- Nouns ending in **-heit, -keit, -schaft, -ung, -ei** are feminine (→**4**)

- Foreign nouns ending in **-anz, -enz, -ie, -ik, -ion, -tät, -ur** are generally feminine (→**5**)

- Nouns denoting the young of a species are neuter (→**6**)

- Infinitives used as nouns are neuter (→**7**)

- Most nouns beginning with **Ge-** are neuter (→**8**)

- **-chen** or **-lein** may be added to many words to give a diminutive form. These words are then neuter (→**9**)
  Note that the vowel adds an umlaut where possible (i.e. on **a, o, u** or **au**) and a final **-e** is dropped before these endings (→**10**)

- Nouns ending in **-nis** or **-tum** are neuter (→**11**)

- Foreign nouns ending in **-at, -ett, -fon, -ma, -ment, -um, -ium** are mainly neuter (→**12**)

- Adjectives and participles may be used as masculine, feminine or neuter nouns (see p 148) (→**13**)

Continued

1 **Er hat eine Drei gekriegt** He got a three (*mark*)
   ein Drittel davon a third of it
2 **die Falte** crease, wrinkle
   die Brücke bridge
3 **der Löwe** lion
   der Matrose sailor
4 **die Eitelkeit** vanity
   die Gewerkschaft trade union
   die Scheidung divorce
   die Druckerei printing works
5 **die Distanz** distance
   die Konkurrenz rivalry
   die Theorie theory
   die Panik panic
   die Union union
   die Elektrizität electricity
   die Partitur score (*musical*)
6 **das Baby** baby
   das Kind child
7 **das Schwimmen** swimming
8 **das Geschirr** crockery, dishes
   das Geschöpf creature
   das Getreide crop
9 **das Kindlein** child
10 **das Bächlein** (small) stream (*from* **der Bach**)
   das Kätzchen kitten (*from* **die Katze**)
11 **das Ereignis** event
   das Altertum antiquity
12 **das Tablett** tray
   das Telefon telephone
   das Testament will
   das Podium platform, podium
13 **der Verwandte** male relative
   die Verwandte female relative
   das Gehackte minced meat

The Gender of Nouns

The following are some common exceptions to the gender guidelines shown on pp 100 to 103

> **das Weib** woman, wife
> **die Person** person
> **die Waise** orphan
> **das Mitglied** member
> **das Genie** genius
> **die Wache** sentry, guard
> **das Restaurant** restaurant

The Formation of Feminine Nouns

As in English, male and female forms are sometimes shown by two completely different words, e.g.

> *mother/father, uncle/aunt etc* (→**1**)

Where such separate forms do not exist, however, German often differentiates between male and female forms in one of two ways:

- The masculine form may sometimes be made feminine by the addition of **-in** in the singular and **-innen** in the plural (→**2**)

- An adjective may be used as a feminine noun (see p 148). It has feminine adjective endings which change according to the article which precedes it (see p 140) (→**3**)

Continued

1 der Vater   **die Mutter**
father   mother
der Bulle   **die Kuh**
bull   cow
der Mann   **die Frau**
man   woman

2 der Lehrer   **die Lehrerin**
(male) teacher   (female) teacher
der König   **die Königin**
king   queen
der Hörer   **die Hörerin**
(male) listener   (female) listener

HENCE:
Liebe Hörer und Hörerinnen! Dear listeners!
unsere Leser und Leserinnen our readers

3 eine Deutsche a German woman
Er ist mit einer Deutschen verheiratet
He is married to a German
die Abgeordnete the female MP
Nur Abgeordnete durften dabeisein
Only MPs were allowed in

The Gender of Nouns: miscellaneous points

Compound Nouns

Compound nouns, i.e. nouns composed of two or more nouns put together, are a regular feature of German.

- They normally take their gender and declension from the last noun of the compound word (→**1**)

- Exceptions to this are compounds ending in **-mut, -scheu** and **-wort**, which do not always have the same gender as the last word when it stands alone (→**2**)

Nouns with more than one gender

- A few nouns have two genders, one of which may only be used in certain regions (→**3**)

- Other nouns have two genders, each of which gives the noun a different meaning (→**4**)

Abbreviations

- These take the gender of their principal noun (→**5**)

1 die **Armbanduhr** wristwatch (*from* die **Uhr**)
  der **Tomatensalat** tomato salad (*from* der **Salat**)
  der **Fußballspieler** footballer (*from* der **Spieler**)

2 der **Mut** courage
  die **Armut** poverty
  die **Demut** humility

  die **Scheu** fear, shyness, timidity
  der **Abscheu** repugnance, abhorrence

  das **Wort** word
  die **Antwort** reply

3 das/der **Radio** radio
  das/der **Keks** biscuit

4 der **Band** volume, book
  das **Band** ribbon, band, tape, bond
  der **See** lake
  die **See** sea
  der **Leiter** leader, manager
  die **Leiter** ladder
  der **Tau** dew
  das **Tau** rope, hawser

5 der **DGB** the Federation of German Trade Unions (*from* der
  Deutsche Gewerkschaftsbund)
  die **EG** the EC (*from* die **Europäische Gemeinschaft**)
  das **AKW** nuclear power station (*from* das **Atomkraftwerk**)

The Cases

There are four grammatical *cases*, which are generally shown by the form of the article used before the noun (see p 118).

The nominative case

- The nominative singular is the form shown in full in dictionary entries. The nominative plural is formed as described on p 98.

- The nominative case is used for:
  - the subject of a verb (→**1**)
  - the complement of **sein** or **werden** (→**2**)

The accusative case

- The noun in the accusative case usually has the same form as in the nominative (→**3**)
  Exceptions to this are "weak" masculine nouns (see p 115) and adjectives used as nouns (see p 148).

- It is used:
  - for the direct object of the verb (→**4**)
  - after those prepositions which always take the accusative case (see p 206 ff) (→**5**)
  - to show change of location after prepositions of place (see p 210) (→**6**)
  - in many expressions of time and place which do not contain a preposition (→**7**)
  - in certain fixed expressions (→**8**)

Continued

1 **Das Mädchen singt** The girl is singing

2 **Er ist ein guter Lehrer** He's a good teacher
   Das wird ein Pullover It's going to be a jumper

3 **das Lied** the song (*nominative*)
   das Lied the song (*accusative*)
   der Wagen the car (*nominative*)
   den Wagen the car (*accusative*)
   die Dose the tin (*nominative*)
   die Dose the tin (*accusative*)

4 **Er hat ein Lied gesungen** He sang a song

5 **für seine Freundin** for his girlfriend
   ohne diesen Wagen without this car
   durch das Rauchen through smoking

6 **in die Stadt** (*accusative*) into town
   BUT:
   in der Stadt (*dative*) in town

7 **Das macht sie jeden Donnerstag**
   She does that every Thursday
   Die Schule ist einen Kilometer entfernt
   The school is a kilometre away

8 **Guten Abend!** Good evening!
   Vielen Dank! Thank you very much!

The Cases (contd)

The genitive case

- In the genitive singular, *masculine* and *neuter* nouns take endings as follows:
  1) **-s** is added to nouns ending in **-en, -el, -er** (→**1**)
  2) **-es** is added to nouns ending in **-tz, -sch, -st** or **-ß** (→**2**)
  3) For nouns of one syllable, either **-s** or **-es** may be added (→**3**)
- *Feminine singular* and all *plural* nouns have the same form as their nominative.
- The genitive is used:
  - to show possession (→**3**)
  - after prepositions taking the genitive (see p 212) (→**4**)
  - in expressions of time when the exact occasion is not specified (→**5**)

The dative case

- Singular nouns in the dative have the same form as in the nominative (→**6**)
- **-e** may be added to the dative singular of *masculine* and *neuter* nouns if the sentence rhythm needs it (→**7**)
  This **-e** is always used in certain set phrases (→**8**)
- Dative plural forms for all genders end in **-n** (→**9**)
  The only exceptions to this are some nouns of foreign origin that end in **-s** in all plural forms, including the dative plural (see p 114) (→**10**)
- The dative is used:
  - as the indirect object (→**11**)
  - after verbs taking the dative (see p 80) (→**12**)
  - after prepositions taking the dative (see p 202) (→**13**)
  - in certain idiomatic expressions (→**14**)
  - instead of the possessive adjective to refer to parts of the body and items of clothing (see p 122) (→**15**)

1 **der Wagen** car → **des Wagens** of the car
  das Rauchen smoking → **des Rauchens** of smoking
  der Computer computer → **des Computers** of the computer
  der Reiter rider → **des Reiters** of the rider

2 **der Sitz** seat; residence → **des Sitzes** of the seat/residence
  der Arzt doctor → **des Arztes** of the doctor
  das Schloß castle → **des Schlosses** of the castle

3 **das Kind** →
  Die Zähne des Kindes waren faul geworden
  The child's teeth had decayed
  Der Name des Kinds war ihm unbekannt
  The child's name was not known to him

4 **wegen seiner Krankheit** because of his illness
  trotz ihrer Bemühungen despite her efforts

5 **eines Tages** one day

6 **dem Wagen** to the car
  der Frau to the woman
  dem Mädchen to the girl

7 **zu welchem Zwecke?** to what purpose?

8 **nach Hause** home
  sich zu Tode trinken/arbeiten
  to drink/work oneself to death

9 **mit den Anwälten** with the lawyers
  nach den Kindern after the children

10 | SINGULAR | PLURAL |
| --- | --- |
| **das Auto** | **die Autos** |
| **das Auto** | **die Autos** |
| **des Autos** | **der Autos** |
| **dem Auto** | **den Autos** |

11 **Er gab dem Mann das Buch** He gave the man the book

12 **Sie half ihrer Mutter** She helped her mother

13 **Nach dem Essen ...** After eating ...

14 **Mir ist kalt** I'm cold

15 **Ich habe mir die Hände gewaschen** I've washed my hands

The Formation of Plurals

The following pages show full noun declensions in all their singular and plural forms.

Those nouns shown represent the most common types of plural.

- Most feminine nouns add **-n, -en** or **-nen** to form their plurals:

	SINGULAR	PLURAL
NOM	**die Frau**	**die Frauen**
ACC	**die Frau**	**die Frauen**
GEN	**der Frau**	**der Frauen**
DAT	**der Frau**	**den Frauen**

- Many nouns have no plural ending.
  These are mainly masculine or neuter nouns ending in **-en, -er, -el**.
  An umlaut is sometimes added to the vowel in the plural forms.

	SINGULAR	PLURAL
NOM	**der Onkel**	**die Onkel**
ACC	**den Onkel**	**die Onkel**
GEN	**des Onkels**	**der Onkel**
DAT	**dem Onkel**	**den Onkeln**

	SINGULAR	PLURAL
NOM	**der Apfel**	**die Äpfel**
ACC	**den Apfel**	**die Äpfel**
GEN	**des Apfels**	**der Äpfel**
DAT	**dem Apfel**	**den Äpfeln**

Continued

The Formation of Plurals (contd)

- Many nouns form their plurals by adding ⸚e

	SINGULAR	PLURAL
NOM	der Stuhl	die Stühle
ACC	den Stuhl	die Stühle
GEN	des Stuhl(e)s	der Stühle
DAT	dem Stuhl(e)	den Stühlen

	SINGULAR	PLURAL
NOM	die Angst	die Ängste
ACC	die Angst	die Ängste
GEN	der Angst	der Ängste
DAT	der Angst	den Ängsten

- Masculine and neuter nouns often add -e in the plural

	SINGULAR	PLURAL
NOM	das Schicksal	die Schicksale
ACC	das Schicksal	die Schicksale
GEN	des Schicksals	der Schicksale
DAT	dem Schicksal(e)	den Schicksalen

- Masculine and neuter nouns sometimes add ⸚er or -er

	SINGULAR	PLURAL
NOM	das Dach	die Dächer
ACC	das Dach	die Dächer
GEN	des Dach(e)s	der Dächer
DAT	dem Dach(e)	den Dächern

Continued

The Formation of Plurals (contd)

Some Unusual Plurals

das Ministerium, die Ministerien department(s)
das Prinzip, die Prinzipien principle(s)
das Thema, die Themen theme(s), topic(s), subject(s)
das Drama, die Dramen drama(s)
die Firma, die Firmen firm(s)
das Konto, die Konten bank account(s)
das Risiko, die Risiken risk(s)
das Komma, die Kommas *or* **Kommata** comma(s); decimal point(s)
das Baby, die Babys baby (babies)
der Klub, die Klubs club(s)
der Streik, die Streiks strike(s)
der Park, die Parks park(s)
der Chef, die Chefs boss(es), chief(s), head(s)
der Israeli, die Israelis Israeli(s)
das Restaurant, die Restaurants restaurant(s)
das Bonbon, die Bonbons sweet(s)
das Hotel, die Hotels hotel(s)
das Niveau, die Niveaus standard(s), level(s)

German singular/English plural nouns

Some nouns are always plural in English, but singular in German:
● Some of the most common examples are:

    eine Brille glasses, spectacles
    eine Schere scissors
    eine Hose trousers

● They are only used in the plural in German to mean more than one pair, e.g. **zwei Hosen** *two pairs of trousers*

The Declension of Nouns (contd)

"Weak" Masculine nouns

Some masculine nouns have a weak declension, which means that in all cases apart from the nominative singular, they end in **-en** or, if the word ends in a vowel, in **-n**

- The dictionary will often show such nouns as
  Junge *m* **-n, -n** boy
  Held *m* **-en, -en** hero

- Weak masculine nouns are declined as follows:

	SINGULAR	PLURAL
NOM	**der Junge**	**die Jungen**
ACC	**den Jungen**	**die Jungen**
GEN	**des Jungen**	**der Jungen**
DAT	**dem Jungen**	**den Jungen**

- Masculine nouns falling into this category include:
  - those ending in **-og(e)** referring to males:
    der Psychologe, der Geologe, der Astrologe
  - those ending in **-aph** or **-oph**:
    der Paragraph, der Philosoph
  - those ending in **-nom** referring to males:
    der Astronom, der Gastronom
  - those ending in **-ant**:
    der Elefant, der Diamant
  - those ending in **-t** which refer to males:
    der Astronaut, der Komponist, der Architekt
  - miscellaneous others:
    der Chirurg, der Bauer, der Ochse, der Kollege, der Spatz, der Mensch, der Katholik, der Franzose

- **der Name** (*name*) has a different ending in the genitive singular, **-ns**: **des Namens**. Otherwise it is the same as **der Junge** shown above. Others in this category are: **der Buchstabe, der Glaube, der Gedanke, der Haufe, der Funke**.

The Declension of Proper Nouns

- Names of people and places add **-s** in the genitive singular unless they are preceded by the definite article or a demonstrative (→**1**)

- Where proper names end in a sibilant (**-s, -sch, -ß, -x, -z, -tz**) and this makes the genitive form with **-s** almost impossible to pronounce, they are best avoided altogether by using **von** followed by the dative case (→**2**)

- Personal names can be given diminutive forms if desired. These may be used as a sign of affection as well as with diminutive meaning (→**3**)

- **Herr** (*Mr*) is always declined where it occurs as part of a proper name (→**4**)

- When articles or adjectives form part of a proper name (e.g. in the names of books, plays, hotels, restaurants *etc*), these are declined in the normal way (see pp 118 and 140) (→**5**)

- Surnames usually form their plurals by adding **-s**, unless they end in a sibilant, in which case they sometimes add **-ens**. They are often preceded by the definite article (→**6**)

Nouns of Measurement and Quantity

- These usually remain singular, even if preceded by a plural number (→**7**)

- The substance which they measure follows in the same case as the noun of quantity, and not in the genitive case as in English (→**8**)

1 **Annas Buch** Anna's book
  Klaras Mantel Klara's coat
  die Werke Goethes Goethe's works
  BUT: **die Versenkung der Bismarck**
  the sinking of the Bismarck

2 **das Buch von Hans** Hans' book
  die Werke von Marx the works of Marx
  die Freundin von Klaus Klaus's girlfriend

3 **von Deinem Sabinchen** from your Sabine
  das kleine Kläuschen hat uns dann ein Lied gesungen
  Then little Klaus sang us a song

4 **an Herrn Schmidt** to Mr Schmidt
  Sehr geehrte Herren Dear Sirs

5 **im Weißen Schwan** in the White Swan
  Er hat den "Zauberberg" schon gelesen
  He has already read "The Magic Mountain"
  nach Karl dem Großen after Charlemagne

6 **Die Schmidts haben uns eingeladen**
  The Schmidts have invited us
  Die Zeißens haben uns eingeladen
  Mr and Mrs Zeiß have invited us

7 **Möchten Sie zwei Stück?**
  Would you like two?

8 **Er wollte zwei Kilo Kartoffeln**
  He wanted two kilos of potatoes
  Sie hat drei Tassen Kaffee getrunken
  She drank three cups of coffee
  Drei Glas Weißwein, bitte!
  Three glasses of white wine please

The Definite Article

In English the definite article *the* always keeps the same form
    the book/*the* books/with *the* books
In German, however, the definite article has many forms:

- In its singular form it changes for masculine, feminine and neuter nouns (→**1**)

- In its plural forms, it is the same for all genders (→**2**)

- The definite article is also used to show the function of the noun in the sentence by showing which case it is.
  There are four cases, as explained more fully on p 108:
    nominative for the subject or complement of the verb (→**3**)
    accusative for the object of the verb and after some prepositions (→**4**)
    genitive to show possession and after some prepositions (→**5**)
    dative for an indirect object (*to* or *for*) and after some prepositions and certain verbs (→**6**)

- The forms of the definite article are as follows:

| | SINGULAR | | | PLURAL |
	MASC	FEM	NEUT	ALL GENDERS
NOM	der	die	das	die
ACC	den	die	das	die
GEN	des	der	des	der
DAT	dem	der	dem	den (→**7**)

Continued

1 *MASCULINE*: **der Mann** the man
                 der Wagen the car
   FEMININE: **die Frau** the wife/woman
                 die Blume the flower
   NEUTER: **das Ding** the thing
                 das Mädchen the girl

2 **die Männer/die Frauen/die Dinge**
   the men/the women/the things

3 **Der Mann ist jung** The man is young
   Die Frau/das Kind ist jung The woman/the child is young

4 **Ich kenne den Mann/die Frau/das Kind**
   I know the man/the woman/the child

5 **der Kopf des Mannes/der Frau/des Kindes**
   the man's/woman's/child's head
   wegen des Mannes/der Frau/des Kindes
   because of the man/the woman/the child

6 **Ich gab es dem Mann/der Frau/dem Kind**
   I gave it to the man/to the woman/to the child

7

		SINGULAR	
	MASC	**FEM**	**NEUT**
NOM	**der Mann**	**die Frau**	**das Kind**
ACC	**den Mann**	**die Frau**	**das Kind**
GEN	**des Mann(e)s**	**der Frau**	**des Kind(e)s**
DAT	**dem Mann(e)**	**der Frau**	**dem Kind(e)**

		PLURAL	
	MASC	**FEM**	**NEUT**
NOM	**die Männer**	**die Frauen**	**die Kinder**
ACC	**die Männer**	**die Frauen**	**die Kinder**
GEN	**der Männer**	**der Frauen**	**der Kinder**
DAT	**den Männern**	**den Frauen**	**den Kindern**

Uses of the Definite Article

When to use and when not to use the definite article in German is one of the most difficult areas for the learner. The following guidelines show where German practice varies from English.

The definite article is used with:

* abstract and other nouns where something is being referred to as a whole or as a general idea (→**1**)
  Where these nouns are quantified or modified, the article is not used (→**2**)

* the genitive, unless the noun is a proper name or is acting as a proper name (→**3**)

* occasionally with proper names to make the sex or case clearer (→**4**)

* always with proper names preceded by an adjective (→**5**)

* sometimes with proper names in familiar contexts or for slight emphasis (→**6**)

* with masculine and feminine countries and districts (→**7**)

* with geographical names preceded by an adjective (→**8**)

* with names of seasons (→**9**)

* often with meals (→**10**)

* with the names of roads (→**11**)

Continued

1 **Das Leben ist schön** Life is wonderful
2 **Es braucht Mut** It needs (some) courage
  Gibt es dort Leben? Is there (any) life there?
3 **das Auto des Lehrers** the teacher's car
  Günters Auto Günter's car
  Muttis Auto Mummy's car
4 **Er hat es Frau Lehmann gegeben**
  Er hat es der Frau Lehmann gegeben
  He gave it to Frau Lehmann
5 **Der alte Herr Brockhaus ist gestorben**
  Old Mr Brockhaus has died
6 **Ich habe heute den Christoph gesehen**
  I saw Christoph today
  Du hast es aber nicht der Petra geschenkt!
  You haven't given it to *Petra*!
7 **Deutschland ist sehr schön** Germany is very beautiful
  Die Schweiz ist auch schön Switzerland is also lovely
8 **im (= in dem) heutigen Deutschland**
  in today's Germany
9 **Im (= in dem) Sommer gehen wir schwimmen**
  We go swimming in summer
  Der Winter kommt bald
  Soon it will be winter
10 **Das Abendessen wird ab acht Uhr serviert**
  Dinner is served from eight o'clock
  Was gibt's zum (= zu dem) Mittagessen?
  What's for lunch?
  BUT:
  Um 8 Uhr ist Frühstück
  Breakfast is at 8 o'clock
11 **Sie wohnt jetzt in der Geisenerstraße**
  She lives in Geisener Road now

Uses of the Definite Article (contd)

- with months of the year except after **seit/nach/vor** (→**1**)

- instead of the possessive adjective to refer to parts of the body and items of clothing (→**2**)
  A reflexive pronoun or noun in the dative case is used if it is necessary to clarify to whom the parts of the body belong (→**3**)

- in expressions of price, to mean *each/per/a* (→**4**)

- with certain common expressions (→**5**)

Others Uses

- The definite article can be used with demonstrative meaning (→**6**)

- After certain prepositions, forms of the definite article can be shortened (see p 198 ff).
  Some of these forms are best used in informal situations (→**7**)
  Others are commonly and correctly used in formal contexts (→**8, 1, 5**)

The definite article may be omitted in German:

- in certain set expressions (→**9**)

- in *preposition + adjective + noun* combinations (→**10**)
  For the declension of adjectives without the article see p 142.

1 **Wir fahren im (= in dem) September weg**
We are going away in September
Wir sind seit September hier
We have been here since September

2 **Er legte den Hut auf den Tisch**
He laid his hat on the table
Ich drücke Ihnen die Daumen I'm keeping my fingers crossed
for you

3 **Er hat sich die Hände schon gewaschen**
He has already washed his hands
Er hat dem Kind schon die Hände gewaschen
He has already washed the child's hands

4 **Die kosten ...**   They cost ...
   ... fünf Mark das Pfund   ... five marks a pound
   ... sechs Mark das Stück ... six marks each

5 **in die Stadt fahren** to go into town
zur (= zu der) Schule gehen to go to school
mit der Post by post
mit dem Zug/Bus/Auto by train/bus/car
im (= in dem) Gefängnis in prison

6 **Du willst das Buch lesen!**
You want to read *that* book!

7 **für das → fürs; vor dem → vorm; um das → ums** *etc*

8 **an dem → am; zu dem → zum; zu der → zur** *etc*

9 **von Beruf** by profession
nach Wunsch as desired
Nachrichten hören to listen to the news

10 **Mit gebeugtem Rücken ...** Bending his back, ...

The Indefinite Article

Like the definite article, the form of the indefinite article varies depending on the gender and case of the noun (→**1**). It has no plural forms (→**2**)

The indefinite article is declined as follows:

	MASC	FEM	NEUT
NOM	ein	eine	ein
ACC	einen	eine	ein
GEN	eines	einer	eines
DAT	einem	einer	einem (→**3**)

- The indefinite article is omitted in the following:

  — descriptions of people by profession, religion, nationality *etc* (→**4**)
  But note that the article is included when an adjective precedes the noun (→**5**)

  — in certain fixed expressions (→**6**)

  — after **als** *as a* (→**7**)

Continued

1 Da ist ein Auto There's a car
Er hat eine Wohnung He has a flat
Sie gab es einem Kind She gave it to a child

2 Autos sind in letzter Zeit teurer geworden
Cars have become more expensive recently

3

	MASC	SINGULAR FEM	NEUT
NOM	ein Mann	eine Frau	ein Kind
ACC	einen Mann	eine Frau	ein Kind
GEN	eines Mann(e)s	einer Frau	eines Kind(e)s
DAT	einem Mann(e)	einer Frau	einem Kind(e)

4 Sie ist Kinderärztin She's a paediatrician
Sie ist Deutsche She's (a) German

5 Sie ist eine sehr geschickte Kinderärztin
She's a very clever paediatrician

6 Es ist Geschmacksache It's a question of taste
Tatsache ist … It's a fact …
Ich habe Kopfschmerzen I've got a headache

7 Als Ausländer ist er hier nicht wahlberechtigt
As a foreigner he doesn't have the vote here
… und ich rede nun als Vater von vier Kindern
… and I'm talking now as a father of four

The Indefinite Article (contd)

In German, a separate negative form of the indefinite article exists. It is declined exactly like **ein** in the singular and also has plural forms:

		SINGULAR		PLURAL
	MASC	FEM	NEUT	ALL GENDERS
NOM	**kein**	**keine**	**kein**	**keine**
ACC	**keinen**	**keine**	**kein**	**keine**
GEN	**keines**	**keiner**	**keines**	**keiner**
DAT	**keinem**	**keiner**	**keinem**	**keinen** (→1)

- It has the meaning *no/not a/not one/not any* (→2)

- It is used even where the equivalent *positive* phrase has no article (→3)

- It is also used in many idiomatic expressions (→4)

- **nicht ein** may be used instead of **kein** where the **ein** is to be emphasized (→5)

1

	MASC	SINGULAR FEM	NEUT
NOM	kein Mann	keine Frau	kein Kind
ACC	keinen Mann	keine Frau	kein Kind
GEN	keines Mann(e)s	keiner Frau	keines Kind(e)s
DAT	keinem Mann(e)	keiner Frau	keinem Kind(e)

		PLURAL	
NOM	keine Männer	keine Frauen	keine Kinder
ACC	keine Männer	keine Frauen	keine Kinder
GEN	keiner Männer	keiner Frauen	keiner Kinder
DAT	keinen Männern	keinen Frauen	keinen Kindern

2 Er hatte keine Geschwister
He had no brothers or sisters
Ich sehe keinen Unterschied I don't see any difference
Das ist keine richtige Antwort That's no answer
Kein Mensch hat es gesehen Not one person has seen it

3 Er hatte Angst davor He was frightened
Er hatte keine Angst davor He wasn't frightened

4 Er hatte kein Geld mehr All his money was gone
Es waren keine drei Monate vergangen, als ...
It was less than three months later that ...
Es hat mich keine zehn Mark gekostet
It cost me less than ten marks

5 Nicht ein Kind hat es singen können
Not *one* child could sing it

Words declined like the Definite Article

The following have endings similar to those of the definite article shown on p 118:

> **jeder, jede, jedes** each, each one, every
> **jener, jene, jenes** that, that one, those
> **dieser, diese, dieses** this, this one, these
> **solcher, solche, solches** such/such a
> **sämtliche** all, entire (*usually plural*)
> **mancher, manche, manches** many a/some
> **einiger, einige, einiges** some, a few, a little
> **welcher, welche, welches** which, which one
> **aller, alle, alles** all, all of them
> **irgendwelcher, -e, -es** some or other
> **beide** both (*plural only*)

- These words can be used as: articles (→1)
  pronouns (→2)

- They have the following endings:

| | SINGULAR | | | PLURAL |
	MASC	FEM	NEUT	ALL GENDERS
NOM	-er	-e	-es	-e
ACC	-en	-e	-es	-e
GEN	-es/-en	-er	-es/-en	-er
DAT	-em	-er	-em	-en

Example declensions are shown on p 134 ff.

- **einiger** and **irgendwelcher** use the **-en** genitive ending before masculine or neuter nouns ending in **-s** (→3)
  jeder, welcher, mancher and **solcher** may also do so (→4)

Continued

1 **Dieser Mann kommt aus Südamerika**
This man comes from South America
Er geht jeden Tag ins Büro
He goes to the office every day
Manche Leute können das nicht
A good many people can't do it

2 **Willst du diesen?** Do you want this one?
In manchem hat er recht He's right about some things
Mann kann ja nicht alles wissen
You can't know everything
Es gibt manche, die keinen Alkohol mögen
There are some people who don't like alcohol

3 **wegen irgendwelchen Geredes**
on account of some gossip

4 **der Besitz solchen Reichtums**
the possession of such wealth
trozt jeden Versuchs
despite all attempts

Words declined like the Definite Article

(contd)

- Adjectives following these words have the weak declension (see p 140) (→**1**)

  Exceptions are the plural forms of **einige**, which are followed by the strong declension (see p 142) (→**2**)

Further points

- **solcher, beide, sämtliche** may be used after another article or possessive adjective. They then take weak (see p 140) or mixed (see p 142) adjectival endings, as appropriate (→**3**)

- Although **beide** generally has plural forms only, one singular form does exist. This is in the neuter nominative and accusative: **beides** (→**4**)

- **dies** often replaces the nominative and accusative **dieses** and **diese** when used as a pronoun (→**5**)

- A fixed form **all** exists which is used together with other articles or possessive pronouns (→**6**)

- **ganz** can also be used to replace both the inflected form **aller/ alle/alles** and the uninflected **all das/dieses/sein** *etc*.

  It is declined as a normal adjective (see p 140) (→**7**)

  It must be used with collective nouns, in time phrases and geographical references (→**8**)

Continued

1 **dieses alte Auto** this old car
aus irgendwelchem dummen Grund
for some stupid reason or other
welche neuen Waren? which new goods?

2 **Dies sind einige gute Freunde von mir**
These are some good friends of mine

3 **Ein solches Kleid habe ich früher auch getragen**
I used to wear a dress like that too
Diese beiden Männer haben es gesehen
Both of these men have seen it

4 **Beides ist richtig** Both are right
Sie hat beides genommen She took both

5 **Hast du dies schon gelesen?**
Have you already read this?
Dies sind meine neuen Sachen
These are my new things

6 **All sein Mut war verschwunden**
All his courage had vanished
mit all diesem Geld with all this money

7 **mit dem ganzen Geld** with all this money

8 **die ganze Gesellschaft** the entire company
Es hat den ganzen Tag geschneit
It snowed the whole day long
Im ganzen Land gab es kein besseres
There wasn't a better one in the whole country

Words declined like the Definite Article
(contd)

- **derjenige/diejenige/dasjenige** (*the one, those*) is declined
  exactly as the definite article plus an adjective in the weak
  declension (see p 140) (→**1**)

- **derselbe/dieselbe/dasselbe** (*the same, the same one*) is
  declined in the same way as **derjenige** (→**2**)

After prepositions, however, the normal contracted forms of the
definite article are used for the appropriate parts of **derselbe** (→**3**)

Continued

1

SINGULAR		
MASC	*FEM*	*NEUT*
der**jenige** Mann	die**jenige** Frau	das**jenige** Kind
den**jenigen** Mann	die**jenige** Frau	das**jenige** Kind
des**jenigen** Mann(e)s	der**jenigen** Frau	des**jenigen** Kind(e)s
dem**jenigen** Mann(e)	der**jenigen** Frau	dem**jenigen** Kind(e)

PLURAL		
MASC	*FEM*	*NEUT*
die**jenigen** Männer	die**jenigen** Frauen	die**jenigen** Kinder
die**jenigen** Männer	die**jenigen** Frauen	die**jenigen** Kinder
der**jenigen** Männer	der**jenigen** Frauen	der**jenigen** Kinder
den**jenigen** Männern	den**jenigen** Frauen	den**jenigen** Kindern

2

SINGULAR		
MASC	*FEM*	*NEUT*
der**selbe** Mann	die**selbe** Frau	das**selbe** Kind
den**selben** Mann	die**selbe** Frau	das**selbe** Kind
des**selben** Mann(e)s	der**selben** Frau	des**selben** Kind(e)s
dem**selben** Mann(e)	der**selben** Frau	dem**selben** Kind(e)

PLURAL		
MASC	*FEM*	*NEUT*
die**selben** Männer	die**selben** Frauen	die**selben** Kinder
die**selben** Männer	die**selben** Frauen	die**selben** Kinder
der**selben** Männer	der**selben** Frauen	der**selben** Kinder
den**selben** Männern	den**selben** Frauen	den**selben** Kindern

3   **zur selben** (= **zu derselben**) **Zeit** at the same time
     im selben (= **in demselben**) **Zimmer** in the same room

Words declined like the Definite Article

(contd)

Sample Declensions in full

dieser, diese, dieses this, this one

		SINGULAR	
	MASC	*FEM*	*NEUT*
NOM	dies**er** Mann	dies**e** Frau	dies**es** Kind
ACC	dies**en** Mann	dies**e** Frau	dies**es** Kind
GEN	dies**es** Mann(e)s	dies**er** Frau	dies**es** Kind(e)s
DAT	dies**em** Mann(e)	dies**er** Frau	dies**em** Kind(e)

		PLURAL	
	MASC	*FEM*	*NEUT*
NOM	dies**e** Männer	dies**e** Frauen	dies**e** Kinder
ACC	dies**e** Männer	dies**e** Frauen	dies**e** Kinder
GEN	dies**er** Männer	dies**er** Frauen	dies**er** Kinder
DAT	dies**en** Männern	dies**en** Frauen	dies**en** Kindern

jener, jene, jenes that, that one

		SINGULAR	
	MASC	*FEM*	*NEUT*
NOM	jen**er** Mann	jen**e** Frau	jen**es** Kind
ACC	jen**en** Mann	jen**e** Frau	jen**es** Kind
GEN	jen**es** Mann(e)s	jen**er** Frau	jen**es** Kind(e)s
DAT	jen**em** Mann(e)	jen**er** Frau	jen**em** Kind(e)

		PLURAL	
	MASC	*FEM*	*NEUT*
NOM	jen**e** Männer	jen**e** Frauen	jen**e** Kinder
ACC	jen**e** Männer	jen**e** Frauen	jen**e** Kinder
GEN	jen**er** Männer	jen**er** Frauen	jen**er** Kinder
DAT	jen**en** Männern	jen**en** Frauen	jen**en** Kindern

jeder, jede, jedes each, every, everybody

	MASC	SINGULAR FEM	NEUT
NOM	jed**er** Wagen	jed**e** Minute	jed**es** Bild
ACC	jed**en** Wagen	jed**e** Minute	jed**es** Bild
GEN	jed**es** Wagens	jed**er** Minute	jed**es** Bild(e)s
	(jed**en** Wagens)		(jed**en** Bild(e)s)
DAT	jed**em** Wagen	jed**er** Minute	jed**em** Bild(e)

welcher, welche, welches which?, which

	MASC	SINGULAR FEM	NEUT
NOM	welch**er** Preis	welch**e** Sorte	welch**es** Mädchen
ACC	welch**en** Preis	welch**e** Sorte	welch**es** Mädchen
GEN	welch**es** Preises	welch**er** Sorte	welch**es** Mädchens
	(welch**en** Preises)		(welch**en** Mädchens)
DAT	welch**em** Preis	welch**er** Sorte	welch**em** Mädchen

	MASC	PLURAL FEM	NEUT
NOM	welch**e** Preise	welch**e** Sorten	welch**e** Mädchen
ACC	welch**e** Preise	welch**e** Sorten	welch**e** Mädchen
GEN	welch**er** Preise	welch**er** Sorten	welch**er** Mädchen
DAT	welch**en** Preisen	welch**en** Sorten	welch**en** Mädchen

Words declined like the Indefinite Article

The following have the same declension pattern as the indefinite articles **ein** and **kein** (see pp 124 and 126):

The possessive adjectives

mein my (→**1**)
dein your (*singular familiar*)
sein his/its
ihr her/its (→**2**)
unser our
euer your (*plural familiar*)
ihr their (→**2**)
Ihr your (*polite singular and plural*)

These words are declined as follows:

	SINGULAR			PLURAL
	MASC	FEM	NEUT	ALL GENDERS
NOM	—	-e	—	-e
ACC	-en	-e	—	-e
GEN	-es	-er	-es	-er
DAT	-em	-er	-em	-en

- Adjectives following these determiners have the mixed declension forms (see p 142), e.g.:

  sein altes Auto   his old car

- **irgendein** *some ... or other* also follows this declension pattern in the singular.
  Its plural form is **irgendwelche** (see p 128).

1 mein, meine, mein my

SINGULAR

	MASC	FEM	NEUT
NOM	mein Bruder	meine Schwester	mein Kind
ACC	meinen Bruder	meine Schwester	mein Kind
GEN	meines Bruders	meiner Schwester	meines Kind(e)s
DAT	meinem Bruder	meiner Schwester	meinem Kind(e)

PLURAL

	MASC	FEM	NEUT
NOM	meine Brüder	meine Schwestern	meine Kinder
ACC	meine Brüder	meine Schwestern	meine Kinder
GEN	meiner Brüder	meiner Schwestern	meiner Kinder
DAT	meinen Brüdern	meinen Schwestern	meinen Kindern

2 ihr, ihre, ihr her/its/their

SINGULAR

	MASC	FEM	NEUT
NOM	ihr Bruder	ihre Schwester	ihr Kind
ACC	ihren Bruder	ihre Schwester	ihr Kind
GEN	ihres Bruders	ihrer Schwester	ihres Kind(e)s
DAT	ihrem Bruder	ihrer Schwester	ihrem Kind(e)

PLURAL

	MASC	FEM	NEUT
NOM	ihre Brüder	ihre Schwestern	ihre Kinder
ACC	ihre Brüder	ihre Schwestern	ihre Kinder
GEN	ihrer Brüder	ihrer Schwestern	ihrer Kinder
DAT	ihren Brüdern	ihren Schwestern	ihren Kindern

Indefinite Adjectives

These are adjectives used in place of, or together with, an article:
    mehrere (*plural only*) several
    viel much, a lot, many
    wenig little, a little, few
    ander other, different

- After the definite article and words declined like it (see p 128) these adjectives have weak declension endings (→**1**)
  Adjectives following the indefinite adjectives are also weak (→**2**)

- After **ein, kein, irgendein** or the possessive adjectives, they have mixed declension endings (→**3**)
  Adjectives following the indefinite adjectives are also mixed in declension (→**4**)

- When used without a preceding article, **ander** and **mehrere** have strong declension endings (→**5**)

- When used without a preceding article, **viel** and **wenig** may be declined as follows, though in the singular they are usually undeclined (→**6**):

| | SINGULAR | | | PLURAL |
	MASC	FEM	NEUT	ALL GENDERS
NOM	**viel**	**viel**	**viel**	**viele**
ACC	**viel**	**viel**	**viel**	**viele**
GEN	**vielen**	**vieler**	**vielen**	**vieler**
DAT	**viel(em)**	**vieler**	**viel(em)**	**vielen**

- Any adjective following **viel** or **wenig** has strong endings (→**7**)

1 Die wenigen Kuchen, die übriggeblieben waren ...
The few cakes which were left over ...

2 Die vielen interessanten Ideen, die ans Licht kamen
The many interesting ideas which came to light

3 Ihr anderes Auto ist in der Werkstatt
Their other car is in for repair

4 Mehrere gute Freunde waren gekommen
Several good friends had come

5 Mehrere prominente Gäste sind eingeladen
Various prominent guests are invited

Er war anderer Meinung
He was of a different opinion

6 Es wurde viel Bier getrunken
They drank a lot of beer

Sie essen nur wenig Obst
They don't eat a lot of fruit

7 Er kaufte viele billige Sachen
He bought a lot of cheap things

Es wurde viel gutes Bier getrunken
They drank a lot of good beer

Sie essen wenig frisches Obst
They don't eat a lot of fresh fruit

The Declension of Adjectives

There are two ways of using adjectives.

- They can be used **attributively**, where the adjective comes before the noun: *the new book*

- They can be used **non-attributively**, where the adjective comes after the verb: *the book is new*

- In English the adjective does not change its form no matter how it is used.
  In German, however, adjectives remain unchanged only when used the second way (non-attributively) (→**1**)
  Used attributively, adjectives change to show the number, gender and case of the noun they precede (→**2**)
  The endings also depend on the nature of the article which precedes them (→**3**)

There are three sets of endings:

1 The weak declension

These are the endings used after **der** and those words declined like it as shown on p 128 (→**4**)

| | SINGULAR | | | PLURAL |
	MASC	FEM	NEUT	ALL GENDERS
NOM	-e	-e	-e	-en
ACC	-en	-e	-e	-en
GEN	-en	-en	-en	-en
DAT	-en	-en	-en	-en

Continued

1 **Das Buch ist neu** The book is new
Der Vortrag war sehr langweilig
The lecture was very boring

2 **Das neue Buch ist da** The new book has arrived
**Während des langweiligen Vortrags sind wir alle einge-
schlafen**
We all fell asleep during the boring lecture

3 **der junge Rechtsanwalt** the young lawyer
ein junger Rechtsanwalt a young lawyer
manch junger Rechtsanwalt many a young lawyer

4

	SINGULAR		
	MASC	FEM	NEUT
NOM	der alte Mann	die alte Frau	das alte Haus
ACC	den alten Mann	die alte Frau	das alte Haus
GEN	des alten Mann(e)s	der alten Frau	des alten Hauses
DAT	dem alten Mann(e)	der alten Frau	dem alten Haus(e)

	PLURAL		
	MASC	FEM	NEUT
NOM	die alten Männer	die alten Frauen	die alten Häuser
ACC	die alten Männer	die alten Frauen	die alten Häuser
GEN	der alten Männer	der alten Frauen	der alten Häuser
DAT	den alten Männern	den alten Frauen	den alten Häusern

The Declension of Adjectives (contd)

2 The mixed declension

These are the endings used after **ein, kein, irgendein** and the possessive adjectives (see p 136) (→**1**):

	SINGULAR			PLURAL
	MASC	FEM	NEUT	ALL GENDERS
NOM	-er	-e	-es	-en
ACC	-en	-e	-es	-en
GEN	-en	-en	-en	-en
DAT	-en	-en	-en	-en　(→**2**)

3 The strong declension

Strong declension endings:

	SINGULAR			PLURAL
	MASC	FEM	NEUT	ALL GENDERS
NOM	-er	-e	-es	-e
ACC	-en	-e	-es	-e
GEN	-en	-er	-en	-er
DAT	-em	-er	-em	-en　(→**3**)

These endings are used where there is no preceding article. The article is omitted more frequently in German than in English, especially in combinations "preposition + adjective + noun" (see p 122).

These endings enable the adjective to do the work of the missing article by showing case, number and gender (→**4**)

Continued

1 Meine neue Stelle ist bei einer großen Druckerei
My new job is with a large printing works
Ihre frühere Theorie ist jetzt bestätigt worden
Her earlier theory has now been proved true

2

	SINGULAR	
MASC	*FEM*	*NEUT*
ein lang**er** Weg	eine lang**e** Reise	ein lang**es** Spiel
einen lang**en** Weg	eine lang**e** Reise	ein lang**es** Spiel
eines lang**en** Wegs	einer lang**en** Reise	eines lang**en** Spieles
einem lang**en** Weg	einer lang**en** Reise	einem lang**en** Spiel

PLURAL
ALL GENDERS

NOM	ihre lang**en** Wege / Reisen / Spiele
ACC	ihre lang**en** Wege / Reisen /Spiele
GEN	ihrer lang**en** Wege / Reisen /Spiele
DAT	ihren lang**en** Wegen / Reisen / Spielen

3

	SINGULAR	
	MASC	*FEM*	*NEUT*
NOM	gut**er** Käse	gut**e** Marmelade	gut**es** Bier
ACC	gut**en** Käse	gut**e** Marmelade	gut**es** Bier
GEN	gut**en** Käses	gut**er** Marmelade	gut**en** Biers
DAT	gut**em** Käse	gut**er** Marmelade	gut**em** Bier

PLURAL
ALL GENDERS

NOM	gut**e** Käse / Marmeladen / Biere
ACC	gut**e** Käse / Marmeladen / Biere
GEN	gut**er** Käse / Marmeladen / Biere
DAT	gut**en** Käsen / Marmeladen / Bieren

4 nach kurzer Fahrt after a short journey
   mit gleichem Gehalt with the same salary

The Declension of Adjectives (contd)

- Strong declension endings are also used after any of the following where they are not preceded by an article or other determiner:

  ein bißchen a little, a bit of
  ein wenig a little
  ein paar a few, a couple (→**1**)
  weniger fewer, less
  einige (*plural forms only*) some
  allerlei/allerhand all kinds of, all sorts of
  keinerlei no … whatsoever, no … at all
  mancherlei various, a number of
  etwas some, any (*singular*) (→**2**)
  mehr more
  lauter nothing but, sheer, pure
  solch such
  vielerlei various, all sorts of, many different
  mehrerlei several kinds of
  was für what, what kind of
  (*note that* **was für ein** *takes the mixed declension*)
  welcherlei what kind of, what sort of
  viel much, many, a lot of
  wievielerlei how many kinds of
  welch! what! what a! (→**3**)
  manch many a
  wenig little, few, not much (→**4**)
  zweierlei/dreierlei *etc* two/three *etc* kinds of
  zwei, drei *etc* two, three *etc* (→**5**)
  (*but note that the mixed declension is used after* **ein**)

- The strong declension is also required after possessives where no other word indicates the case, gender and number (→**6**)

Continued

1 ein paar gute Tips (*strong declension*)
a couple of good tips

2 Etwas starken Pfeffer zugeben (*strong*)
Add a little strong pepper

3 Welch herrliches Wetter! (*strong*)
What splendid weather!

4 Es gab damals nur wenig frisches Obst (*strong*)
At that time there was little fresh fruit
BUT:
Das wenige frische Obst, das es damals gab ... (*weak*)
The little fresh fruit that was then available ...

5 Zwei große Jungen waren gekommen (*strong*)
Two big boys had come along
BUT:
Die zwei großen Jungen, die gekommen waren (*weak*)
The two big boys who had come along
Meine zwei großen Jungen (*mixed*)
My two big sons

6 Herberts altes Buch (*strong*)
Herbert's old book

Muttis neues Auto (*strong*)
Mum's new car

The Declension of Adjectives (contd)

Some spelling changes when adjectives are declined

- When the adjective **hoch** (*high*) is declined, its stem changes to **hoh-** (→1)

- Adjectives ending in **-el** lose the **-e-** of their stem when inflected, i.e. when endings are added (→2)

- Adjectives with an **-er** ending often lose the **-e-** from the ending when inflected (→3)

The participles as adjectives

- The present participle can be used as an adjective with normal adjectival endings (pp 140 to 143) (→4)
  The present participles of **sein** and **haben** cannot be used in this way

- The past participle can also be used as an adjective in this way (→5)

Adjectives followed by the dative case

A *dative case* is required after many adjectives e.g. (→6):
  ähnlich similar to
  bekannt familiar to
  dankbar grateful to
  fremd alien to
  gleich all the same to; like
  leicht easy for
  nah close to
  peinlich painful for
  unbekannt unknown to

1 **Das Gebäude ist hoch** The building is high
   BUT:
   ein hohes Gebäude a high building

2 **Das Zimmer ist dunkel** The room is dark
   BUT:
   in dem dunklen Zimmer in the dark room

3 **Das Auto war teuer** The car was expensive
   BUT:
   Er kaufte ein teures Auto He bought an expensive car

4 **die werdende Mutter** the mother-to-be
   ein lachendes Kind a laughing child

5 **meine verlorenen Sachen** my lost things
   die ausgebeuteten Arbeiter
   the exploited workers

6 **Ist dir das bekannt?** Do you know about it?
   Ich wäre Ihnen dankbar, wenn ...
   I should be grateful to you if ...
   Diese Sache ist mir etwas peinlich
   This matter is somewhat embarrassing for me
   Solche Gedanken waren ihm fremd
   Such thoughts were alien to him

Adjectives used as nouns

All adjectives in German, and those participles used as adjectives, can also be used as nouns. These are often called **adjectival nouns**

- Adjectives and participles used as nouns have:
  a capital letter like other nouns (→**1**)
  declension endings like other adjectives, depending on the preceding article, if any (see below) (→**2**)

Declension endings for adjectives used as nouns:

- after **der, dieser** and words like it shown on p 128, the normal *weak* adjective endings apply (see p 140) (→**3**)
  Der Junge (*the boy*) is an exception and is declined like a weak masculine noun, as shown on p 115.

- after **ein, kein, irgendein** and the possessive adjectives shown on p 136, the *mixed* adjective endings apply (see p 142) (→**4**)

- where no article is present, or after those words shown on p 144, the *strong* adjective endings are used (see p 142) (→**5**)
  When another adjective precedes the adjectival noun, the *strong* endings become *weak* in two instances:

  in the *dative singular* (→**6**)

  in the *nominative and accusative plural* after a possessive, where the strong endings might cause confusion with the singular feminine form (→**7**)

- Some adjectival nouns have become part of set expressions, and these tend to be written without the capital letter (→**8**)

1 der Angestellte the employee

2 die Angestellte the female employee
das Neue daran ist ... the new thing about it is ...

3 für den Angeklagten for the accused
mit dieser Bekannten with this (*female*) friend

4 Kein Angestellter darf hier rauchen
No employee may smoke here
Sie machten einen Ausflug mit ihren Bekannten zusammen
They went on a trip with their friends

5 Etwas Besonderes ist geschehen
Something special has happened

6 Ich hatte es Rudis jüngerem Verwandten versprochen
I had promised it to Rudi's young relative

7 Rudis jüngere Verwandten wollten es haben
Rudi's young relatives wanted to have it

8 Es bleibt beim alten Things remain as they were
Er hat den ersten besten genommen
He took the first that came to hand

Miscellaneous points

Adjectives of nationality

- These are not spelt with a capital letter in German except in public or official names (→**1**)

- However, when used as a noun to refer to the language, a capital is used (→**2**)

- In German, for expressions like *he is English/he is German etc* a noun or adjectival noun is used instead of an adjective (→**3**)

Adjectives derived from place names

- These are formed by adding **-er** to names of towns (→**4**)

- They are never inflected (→**5**)

- Adjectives from **die Schweiz** and from certain regions can also be formed in this way (→**6**)

- Such adjectives may be used as nouns denoting the inhabitants of a town.
  They are then declined as normal nouns (see p 98ff) (→**7**) The feminine form is made by adding **-in** in the singular and **-innen** in the plural (→**8**)

- Certain names ending in **-en** drop the **-e-** or the **-en** of their ending before adding **-er** (→**9**)

- A second type of adjective formed from place names exists, ending in **-isch** and spelt with a small letter. It is inflected as a normal adjective (see p 140).
  It is used mainly where the speaker is referring to the mood of, or something typical of, that place (→**10**)

1 **die deutsche Sprache** the German language
das französische Volk the French people
BUT **die Deutsche Bundesbahn**

2 **Sie sprechen kein Englisch** They don't speak English

3 **Er ist Deutscher** He is German
Sie ist Deutsche She is German

4 **Kölner, Frankfurter, Leipziger** *etc*

5 **der Kölner Dom** Cologne cathedral
ein Frankfurter Würstchen a frankfurter sausage

6 **Schweizer Käse** Swiss cheese

7 **Die Sprache des Kölners heißt Kölsch**
von den Frankfurtern

8 **Die Kölnerin, die Kölnerinnen**
Die Londonerin, die Londonerinnen

9 **München** → **der Münchner**
Bremen → **der Bremer**
Göttingen → **der Göttinger**

10 **ein echt frankfurterischer Ausdruck**
a real Frankfurt expression
Er spricht etwas münchnerisch
He has something of a Munich accent

The Comparison of Adjectives

Adjectives have three basic forms of comparison:

A simple form used to describe something or someone:

e.g. a *little* house/the house is *little*

● This form is fully dealt with on pp 140 to 147.

● Simple forms are used in *as ... as / not as ... as* comparisons (→**1**)

A comparative form used to compare two things or persons:

e.g. he is *bigger* than his brother

● In German, comparatives are formed by adding **-er** to the simple form (→**2**)

● *than* in comparative statements is translated by **als** (→**3**)

● Unlike English, the vast majority of German adjectives, including those of several syllables, form their comparatives in this way (→**4**)

● Many adjectives modify the stem vowel when forming their comparatives, as in the common examples shown opposite (→**5**)

Continued

1 so ... wie as ... as:
Er ist so gut wie sein Bruder
He is as good as his brother

ebenso ... wie just as ... as:
Er war ebenso glücklich wie ich
He was just as happy as I was

zwei-/dreimal *etc* **so ... wie**
twice/three *etc* times as ... as:
Er war zweimal so groß wie sein Bruder
He was twice as big as his brother

nicht so ... wie not as ... as:
Er ist nicht so alt wie du
He is not as old as you

2 klein / kleiner   small / smaller
schön / schöner   lovely / lovelier

3 Er ist kleiner als seine Schwester
He is smaller than his sister

4 bequem / bequemer   comfortable / more comfortable
gebildet / gebildeter   educated / more educated
effektiv / effektiver   effective / more effective

5 alt / älter   old / older
stark / stärker   strong / stronger
schwach / schwächer   weak / weaker
scharf / schärfer   sharp / sharper
lang / länger   long / longer
kurz / kürzer   short / shorter
warm / wärmer   warm / warmer
kalt / kälter   cold / colder
hart / härter   hard / harder
groß / größer   big / bigger

Comparison of Adjectives (contd)

- Adjectives whose simple form ends in **-el** lose the **-e-** before adding the comparative ending **-er** (→**1**)

- Adjectives with a diphthong followed by **-er** in their simple forms also drop the **-e-** before adding **-er** (→**2**)

- Adjectives whose simple form ends in **-en** or **-er** may drop the **-e-** of the simple form when adjectival endings are added to their comparative forms (→**3**)

- With a few adjectives, comparative forms may be used not only for comparison, but also to render the idea of "-ish" or "rather …"
  Some common examples are:

älter elderly	**dünner** thinnish
größer largish	**kürzer** shortish
kleiner smallish	**jünger** youngish
dicker fattish	**neuer** newish (→**4**)

- When used attributively (*before* the noun), comparative forms are declined in exactly the same way as simple adjectives (see pp 140 to 147) (→**4, 5**)

A superlative form used to compare three or more persons or things:

e.g. he is *the biggest/the best*

- Superlatives are formed by adding **-st** to the simple adjective. The vowel is modified, as for comparative forms, where applicable.
  Superlative forms are generally used with an article and take endings accordingly (see p 140) (→**6**)

Continued

1 **eitel / eitler** vain / vainer
dunkel / dunkler dark / darker

2 **sauer / saurer** sour / more sour
die saurere Zitrone the sourer lemon
Der Wein ist saurer geworden
The wine has grown more sour
teuer / teurer expensive / more expensive
Das ist eine teurere Sorte
That is a more expensive kind
Die Neuen sind teurer
The new ones are more expensive

3 **finster / finsterer** dark / darker
ein finstreres Gesicht
OR
ein finstereres Gesicht
a grimmer face

4 **ein älterer Herr** an elderly gentleman
eine größere Summe a rather large sum
von jüngerem Aussehen of youngish appearance

5 **Die jüngere Schwester ist größer als die ältere**
The younger sister is bigger than the older one
Mein kleinerer Bruder geht jetzt zur Schule
My younger brother goes to school now

6 **Er ist der Jüngste** He is the youngest
Ihr erfolgreichster Versuch war im Herbst 1990
Her most successful attempt was in the autumn of 1990

Comparison of Adjectives (contd)

- Many adjectives form their superlative forms by adding **-est** instead of **-st** where pronunciation would otherwise be difficult or unaesthetic (→**1**)

- The English superlative *most* meaning *very* can be shown in German by any of the following (→**2**):

  äußerst
  sehr
  besonders
  außerordentlich
  höchst (not with monosyllabic words)
  furchtbar (conversational only)
  richtig (conversational only)

Some irregular comparative and superlative forms

SIMPLE FORM	COMPARATIVE	SUPERLATIVE
gut	**besser**	**der beste**
hoch	**höher**	**der höchste**
viel	**mehr**	**der meiste**
nah	**näher**	**der nächste**

1 **der/die/das schlechteste** the worst
der/die/das schmerzhafteste the most painful
der/die/das süßeste the sweetest
der/die/das neueste the newest
der/die/das stolzeste the proudest
der/die/das frischeste the freshest

2 **Er ist ein äußerst begabter Mensch**
He is a most gifted person

Das Essen war besonders schlecht
The food was really/most dreadful

Der Wein war furchtbar teuer!
The wine was dreadfully/most expensive!

Das sieht richtig komisch aus
That looks really/most funny

Personal Pronouns

As in English, personal pronouns change their form depending on their function in the sentence:

I saw *him* / *He* saw *me* / *We* saw *her* (→**1**)

The personal pronouns are declined as follows (→**2**):

NOMINATIVE	ACCUSATIVE	DATIVE
ich I	**mich** me	**mir** to/for me
du you	**dich** you	**dir** to/for you
er he/it	**ihn** him/it	**ihm** to/for him/it
sie she/it	**sie** her/it	**ihr** to/for her/it
es it/he/she	**es** it/him/her	**ihm** to/for it/him/her
wir we	**uns** us	**uns** to/for us
ihr you (*plural*)	**euch** you	**euch** to/for you
sie they	**sie** them	**ihnen** to/for them
Sie you (*polite*)	**Sie** you	**Ihnen** to/for you
man one	**einen** one	**einem** to/for one

- As can be seen from the above table, there are three ways of addressing people in German, by **du, ihr** or **Sie.**
  All three forms are illustrated overleaf.

- Personal pronouns in the dative require no preposition when acting as indirect object, i.e. *to* me, *to* him *etc* (→**3**)

Continued

1 **Ich sah ihn** I saw him
  Er sah mich He saw me
  Wir sahen sie We saw her

2 **Wir sind mit ihnen spazierengegangen**
  We went for a walk with them
  Sie haben uns eine tolle Geschichte erzählt
  They told us a great story
  Soll ich Ihnen etwas mitbringen?
  Shall I bring something back for you?

3 **Er hat es ihr gegeben**
  He gave it to her
  Ich habe ihm ein neues Buch gekauft
  I bought a new book for him/I bought him a new book

Personal Pronouns (contd)

- **du** is a singular form, used only when speaking to one person. It is used to talk to children, close friends and relatives, animals and objects of affection such as a toy, one's car etc.
  When in doubt it is always best to use the more formal **Sie** form.

- **ihr** is simply the plural form of **du** and is used in exactly the same situations wherever more than one person is to be addressed (→**1**)

- The familiar forms and their possessives are usually written with a small letter (→**2**)
  In letters, however, they must begin with a capital letter (→**3**)

- **Sie** is the polite, or formal, way of addressing people. It is written in all its declined forms with a capital letter, including the possessive (→**4**)

  Sie is used:
  a) by children talking to adults outside their immediate family
  b) by adults talking to older children from mid-teens onwards. Teachers use it to their senior classes and bosses to their trainees etc.
  c) among adult strangers meeting for the first time
  d) among colleagues, friends and acquaintances unless a suggestion has been formally made by one party and accepted by the other that the familiar forms should be used. Familiar forms must then continue to be used at all times, as a reversion to the formal might be considered insulting.

Continued

1 Kinder, was wollt ihr essen?
Children, what do you want to eat?

2 Er hat mir gesagt, du sollst deine Frau mitbringen
He told me you were to bring your wife

3 Liebe Elke,
Gestern bin ich Deinem Bruder begegnet. Er wollte wissen, warum Du nichts von Dir hören läßt!
Dear Elke,
I met your brother yesterday. He was wondering why you haven't been in touch!

4 Was haben Sie gesagt?
What did you say?

Ich habe es Ihnen schon gegeben
I have already given it to you

Ja, Ihre Sachen sind jetzt fertig
Yes, your things are ready now

Personal Pronouns (contd)

er/sie/es

All German nouns are masculine, feminine or neuter (→1)
The personal pronoun must agree in number and in gender with
the noun which it represents.

> **es** is used only for neuter nouns, and not for all inanimate
> objects (→2)
> Inanimate objects which are masculine use the pronoun **er**
> (→3)
> Feminine inanimate objects use the pronoun **sie** (→4)
> Neuter nouns referring to people have the neuter pronoun
> **es** (→5)

A common error for English speakers is to call all objects **es**.

man

This is used in much the same way as the pronoun **one** in English,
but it is much more commonly used in German (→6)
It is also used to make an alternative passive form (see p 34) (→7)

The genitive personal pronoun

Genitive forms of the personal pronouns do exist (→8)
In practice, however, these are rarely used. Wherever possible,
alternative expressions are found which do not require the genitive
personal pronoun.

Special genitive forms exist for use with the prepositions **wegen**
and **willen** (→9)

Continued

1 der **Tisch** the table (*masculine*)
die **Gardine** the curtain (*feminine*)
das **Baby** the baby (*neuter*)

2 **Das Bild ist schön** → **Es ist schön**
The picture is beautiful → It is beautiful

3 **Der Tisch ist groß** → **Er ist groß**
The table is large → It is large

4 **Die Gardine ist weiß** → **Sie ist weiß**
The curtain is white → It is white

5 **Das Kind stand auf** → **Es stand auf**
The child stood up → He/she stood up

6 **Es tut einem gut** It does one good

7 **Man holt mich um sieben ab**
I am being picked up at seven

8
meiner	of me	**unser**	of us
deiner	of you	**euer**	of you (*plural*)
seiner	of him/of it	**ihrer**	of them
ihrer	of her/it	**Ihrer**	of you (*polite*)

9 **meinetwegen** because of me, on my account
deinetwegen because of you, on your account *etc*
seinetwegen
ihretwegen
unsertwegen
euretwegen
Ihretwegen

meinetwillen for my sake, for me *etc*
deinetwillen
ihretwillen *etc*

Personal Pronouns (contd)

The use of pronouns after prepositions

- Personal pronouns used after prepositions and referring to a person are in the *case* required by the preposition in question (see p 198 ff) (→**1**)

- When, however, a *thing* rather than a person is referred to, the construction:

    preposition + pronoun

    becomes:

    da- + *preposition* (→**2**) Before a preposition beginning with a vowel, the form: **dar-** + *preposition* is used (→**3**)

    This affects the following prepositions:

an	**auf**	**aus**
bei	**durch**	**für**
in	**mit**	**nach**
neben	**über**	**unter**
zwischen		

- These contracted forms are used after verbs followed by a preposition (see p 76 ff) (→**4**)

- After prepositions used to express motion the form with **da(r)-** is not felt to be sufficiently strong. Forms with **hin** and **her** are used as follows:

    aus : heraus / hinaus
    auf : herauf / hinauf
    in : herein / hinein (→**5**)

1 Ich bin mit ihm spazierengegangen
I went for a walk with him

**2 Klaus hatte ein Messer geholt und wollte damit den Kuchen
schneiden**
Klaus had brought a knife and was about to cut the cake with it

3 Lege es bitte darauf
Put it there please

4 Der Unterschied liegt darin, daß ...
The difference is that ...
Ich erinnere mich nicht daran
I don't remember (it)

5 Er sah eine Treppe und ging leise hinauf
He saw some stairs and climbed them quietly
Endlich fand er unser Zelt und kam herein
He finally found our tent and came in
Er öffnete den Koffer und legte das Hemd hinein
He opened his suitcase and put in his shirt

Possessive Pronouns

>**meiner** mine
>**deiner** yours
>**seiner** his/its
>**ihrer** hers/its
>**uns(e)rer** ours
>**eu(e)rer** yours (*plural*)
>**ihrer** theirs
>**Ihrer** yours (*polite form*)

These have the same endings as **dieser**. Their declension is therefore the same as for possessive adjectives (see p 136) except in the masculine nominative singular and the neuter nominative and accusative singular:

	MASC	SINGULAR FEM	NEUT	PLURAL ALL GENDERS
NOM	-er	-e	-(e)s	-e
ACC	-en	-e	-(e)s	-e
GEN	-es	-er	-es	-er
DAT	-em	-er	-em	-en

● The bracketed (**e**) is often omitted, especially in spoken German

● Possessive pronouns must agree in number, gender and case with the noun they replace (→**1**)

● Note the translation of *of mine, of yours* etc (→**2**)

● **meiner** is declined in full opposite (→**3**)
  Like **meiner** are **deiner, seiner** and **ihrer**.
  Unserer and **euerer** are shown in full, since they have slightly different forms with an optional **-e-** (→**4**)

Continued

1 Der Wagen da drüben ist meiner. Er ist kleiner als deiner
The car over there is mine. It is smaller than yours

2 Er ist ein Bekannter von mir
He is an acquaintance of mine

3 meiner mine

| | SINGULAR | | | PLURAL |
	MASC	FEM	NEUT	ALL GENDERS
NOM	meiner	meine	mein(e)s	meine
ACC	meinen	meine	mein(e)s	meine
GEN	meines	meiner	meines	meiner
DAT	meinem	meiner	meinem	meinen

4 uns(e)rer ours

| | SINGULAR | | | PLURAL |
	MASC	FEM	NEUT	ALL GENDERS
NOM	uns(e)rer	uns(e)re	uns(e)res	uns(e)re
ACC	uns(e)ren	uns(e)re	uns(e)res	uns(e)re
GEN	uns(e)res	uns(e)rer	uns(e)res	uns(e)rer
DAT	uns(e)rem	uns(e)rer	uns(e)rem	uns(e)ren

eu(e)rer yours (*plural*)

| | SINGULAR | | | PLURAL |
	MASC	FEM	NEUT	ALL GENDERS
NOM	eu(e)rer	eu(e)re	eu(e)res	eu(e)re
ACC	eu(e)ren	eu(e)re	eu(e)res	eu(e)re
GEN	eu(e)res	eu(e)rer	eu(e)res	eu(e)rer
DAT	eu(e)rem	eu(e)rer	eu(e)rem	eu(e)ren

Possessive Pronouns (contd)

Alternative forms

There are two alternatives to the **meiner/deiner** *etc* forms shown on p 167:

- **der, die, das meinige** mine
  der, die, das deinige yours
  der, die, das seinige his/its
  der, die, das ihrige hers/its
  der, die, das uns(e)rige ours
  der, die, das eu(e)rige yours (*plural*)
  der, die, das ihrige theirs
  der, die, das Ihrige yours (*polite form*)

  These are not as common as the **meiner/deiner** *etc* forms (→**1**)

  These forms are declined as the definite article plus a weak adjective (see p 140) (→**2**)

  The bracketed (**e**) of the first and second person plural is often omitted in spoken German.

- **der, die, das meine** mine
  der, die, das deine yours
  der, die, das seine his/its
  der, die, das ihre hers/its
  der, die, das uns(e)re ours
  der, die, das eu(e)re yours (*plural*)
  der, die, das ihre theirs
  der, die, das Ihre yours (*polite form*)

  These forms are also less common than the **meiner/deiner** *etc* forms. They are declined as the definite article followed by a weak adjective (→**3**)

1 Ihr Auto ist aber neuer als das meinige
Your car is newer than mine
Paul hat seiner Freundin Blumen gekauft. Ich habe der meinigen Parfüm geschenkt
Paul bought his girlfriend some flowers. I bought mine perfume

2

	MASC	SINGULAR FEM	NEUT
NOM	der meinige	die meinige	das meinige
ACC	den meinigen	die meinige	das meinige
GEN	des meinigen	der meinigen	des meinigen
DAT	dem meinigen	der meinigen	dem meinigen

	PLURAL ALL GENDERS
NOM	die meinigen
ACC	die meinigen
GEN	der meinigen
DAT	den meinigen

3

	MASC	SINGULAR FEM	NEUT
NOM	der meine	die meine	das meine
ACC	den meinen	die meine	das meine
GEN	des meinen	der meinen	des meinen
DAT	dem meinen	der meinen	dem meinen

	PLURAL ALL GENDERS
NOM	die meinen
ACC	die meinen
GEN	der meinen
DAT	den meinen

Reflexive Pronouns

Reflexive pronouns, used to form reflexive verbs, have two forms, accusative and dative, as follows (→1)

ACCUSATIVE	DATIVE	
mich	**mir**	myself
dich	**dir**	yourself
sich	**sich**	himself/herself/itself/themselves
uns	**uns**	ourselves
euch	**euch**	yourselves
sich	**sich**	yourself/yourselves (*polite forms*)

- Unlike personal pronouns and possessives, the polite forms have no capital letter (→2)

- For the position of reflexive pronouns within a sentence see p 30 (reflexive verbs) and pp 224 to 235 (sentence structure).

- Reflexive pronouns are also used after prepositions when the pronoun has the function of "reflecting back" to the subject of the sentence (→3)

- A further use of reflexive pronouns in German is with transitive verbs where the action is performed for the benefit of the subject, as in the English phrase:

      I bought *myself* a new hat

  The pronoun is not always translated in English (→4)

Continued

1 **Er hat sich rasiert** He had a shave
  Du hast dich gebadet You had a bath
  Ich will es mir zuerst überlegen
  I'll have to think about it first

2 **Setzen Sie sich bitte** Please take a seat

3 **Er hatte nicht genug Geld bei sich** (*NOT* **bei ihm**)
  He didn't have enough money on him

4 **Ich hole mir ein Bier**
  I'm going to get a beer (for myself)
  Er hat sich einen neuen Anzug gekauft
  He bought (himself) a new suit

Reflexive Pronouns (contd)

- Reflexive pronouns may be used for *reciprocal* actions, usually rendered by "each other" in English (→**1**)

  Reciprocal actions may also be expressed by **einander**.
  This does not change in form (→**2**)

  einander is always used in place of the reflexive pronoun after prepositions. Note that the preposition and **einander** come together to form one word (→**3**)

Emphatic reflexive pronouns

In English, these have the same forms as the normal reflexive pronouns:
> The queen *herself* has given the order
> I haven't read it *myself*, but …

In German, this idea is expressed not by the reflexive pronouns, but by **selbst** or (in colloquial speech) **selber** placed at some point in the sentence after the noun or pronoun to which they refer (→**4**)

- **selbst/selber** do not change their form, regardless of number and gender of the noun to which they refer (→**4**)

- They are always stressed, regardless of their position in the sentence.

1 **Wir sind uns letzte Woche begegnet**
We met (each other) last week
Sie hatten sich auf einer Tagung kennengelernt
They had got to know each other at a conference

2 **Wir kennen uns schon**
OR:
Wir kennen einander schon
We already know each other

Sie kennen sich schon
OR:
Sie kennen einander schon
They already know each other

3 **Sie redeten miteinander**
They were talking to each other

4 **Die Königin selbst hat es befohlen**
The queen herself has given the order
Ich selbst habe es nicht gelesen, aber ...
I haven't read it myself, but ...

Relative Pronouns

These have the same forms as the definite article, except in the dative plural and genitive cases.

They are declined as follows:

| | SINGULAR | | | PLURAL |
	MASC	FEM	NEUT	ALL GENDERS
NOM	der	die	das	die
ACC	den	die	das	die
GEN	dessen	deren	dessen	deren
DAT	dem	der	dem	denen

- Relative pronouns must agree in gender and number with the noun to which they refer. They take their case however from the function they have in their own relative clause (→**1**)

- The relative pronoun cannot be omitted in German as it sometimes is in English (→**2**)

- The genitive forms are used in relative clauses in much the same way as in English (→**3**)
  Note however the translation of certain phrases (→**4**)

- When a preposition introduces the relative clause, the relative pronoun may be replaced by **wo-** or **wor-** if the noun or pronoun it stands for refers to an inanimate object or abstract concept (→**5**)
  The full form of relative pronoun plus preposition is however stylistically better.

- Relative clauses are always divided off by commas from the rest of the sentence (→**1-5**)

Continued

1 **Der Mann, den ich gestern gesehen habe, kommt aus Hamburg**
The man whom I saw yesterday comes from Hamburg

2 **Die Frau, mit der ich gestern gesprochen habe, kennt deine Mutter**
The woman I spoke to yesterday knows your mother

3 **Das Kind, dessen Fahrrad gestohlen worden war, ...**
The child whose bicycle had been stolen ...

4 **Die Kinder, von denen einige schon lesen konnten, ...**
The children, some of whom could read, ...
Meine Freunde, von denen einer ...
My friends, one of whom ...

5 **Das Buch, woraus ich vorgelesen habe, ...**
OR:
Das Buch, aus dem ich vorgelesen habe, ...
The book I read aloud from ...

Relative Pronouns (contd)

welcher

A second relative pronoun exists. This has the same forms as the interrogative adjective **welcher** without the genitive forms:

| | | SINGULAR | | PLURAL |
	MASC	FEM	NEUT	ALL GENDERS
NOM	**welcher**	**welche**	**welches**	**welche**
ACC	**welchen**	**welche**	**welches**	**welche**
GEN	—	—	—	—
DAT	**welchem**	**welcher**	**welchem**	**welchen**

- These forms are used only infrequently as relative pronouns, where sentence rhythm might benefit.

- They are also useful used as articles or adjectives to connect a noun in the relative clause with the contents of the main clause (→**1**)

wer, was

These are normally used as interrogative pronouns meaning *who?, what?* and are declined as such on p 178.

- They may, however, also be used without interrogative meaning to replace both subject and relative pronoun in English:
  he who, a woman who, anyone who, those who etc (→**2**)

- **was** is the relative pronoun used in set expressions with certain neuter forms (→**3**)

1 **Er glaubte, mit der Hausarbeit nicht helfen zu brauchen, mit welcher Idee seine Mutter nicht einverstanden war!**
He thought he didn't have to help in the house, an idea with which his mother was not in agreement!

2 **Wer das glaubt, ist verrückt**
Anyone who believes that is mad
Was mich angeht, ... For my part ...
Was du gestern gekauft hast, steht dir ganz gut
The things you bought yesterday suit you very well

3 **nichts, was ...** nothing that
vieles, was ... a lot that
einiges, was ... some that
dasselbe, was ... the same one that
wenig, was ... little that
dasjenige, was ... that which
folgendes, was ... the following which
manches, was ... some which
allerlei, was ... all kinds of things that
alles, was ... everything which
das, was ... that which

Nichts, was er sagte, hat gestimmt
Nothing that he said was right
Das, was du jetzt machst, ist reiner Unsinn!
What you are doing now is sheer nonsense!
Mit allem, was du gesagt hast, sind wir einverstanden
We agree with everything you said

Interrogative Pronouns

These are the pronouns used to ask questions.

As in English, they have few forms, singular and plural being the same.

They are declined as follows:

	PERSONS	THINGS
	PERSONS	*THINGS*
NOM	**wer?**	**was?**
ACC	**wen?**	**was?**
GEN	**wessen?**	**wessen?**
DAT	**wem?**	—

- They are used in direct questions   (→**1**)
           or in indirect questions   (→**2**)

- When used as the subject of a sentence, they are always followed by a singular verb (→**3**)
  EXCEPTION:
  When followed by a verb and taking a noun complement, the verb may be plural if the sense demands it (→**4**)

- The interrogative pronouns can be used in rhetorical questions or in exclamations (→**5**)

Continued

1 **Wer hat es gemacht?** Who did it?
   Mit wem bist du gekommen?
   Who did you come with?

2 **Ich weiß nicht, wer es gemacht hat**
   I don't know who did it
   Er wollte wissen, mit wem er fahren sollte
   He wanted to know who he was to travel with

3 **Wer kommt heute?** Who's coming today?

4 **Wer sind diese Leute?** Who are these people?

5 **Was haben wir gelacht!** How we laughed!

Interrogative Pronouns (contd)

- When used with prepositions, **was** usually becomes **wo-** and is placed in front of the preposition to form one word with it (→**1**)
  Where the preposition begins with a vowel, **wor-** is used instead (→**2**)
  This construction is similar to **da(r)-** + *preposition* shown on p 164

  As with **da(r)-** + *preposition,* this construction is not used when the preposition is intended to convey movement.
  Wohin (*where to*) and **woher** (*where from*) are used instead (→**3**)

was für ein?, welcher?

- These are used to mean *what kind of one?* and *which one?*

- They are declined as shown on pp 124 and 128.

- They are used to form either direct or indirect questions (→**4**)

- They may refer either to persons or to things with the appropriate declension endings (→**5**)

1 Wonach sehnst du dich? What do you long for?
Wodurch ist es zerstört worden?
How was it destroyed?

2 Worauf kann man sich heutzutage noch verlassen?
What is there left to rely on these days?

3 Wohin fährst du? Where are you going?
Woher kommt das?
Where has this come from?/How has this come about?

4 Was für eins hat er?
What kind (of one) does he have?
Welches hast du gewollt?
Which one did you want?

5 Für welchen hat sie sich entschieden?
Which one (*man/hat etc*) did she choose?

Indefinite Pronouns

jemand someone, somebody

NOM	**jemand**
ACC	**jemanden, jemand**
GEN	**jemand(e)s**
DAT	**jemandem, jemand** (→1)

niemand no-one, nobody

NOM	**niemand**
ACC	**niemanden, niemand**
GEN	**niemand(e)s**
DAT	**niemandem, niemand** (→2)

- The forms without endings are used in conversational German, but the inflected forms are preferred in literary and written styles.

- When **niemand** and **jemand** are used with a following adjective, they are usually not declined, but the adjective takes a capital letter and is declined as follows:

NOM	**jemand/niemand Neues**
ACC	**jemand/niemand Neues**
GEN	—
DAT	**jemand/niemand Neuem** (→3)

- When **jemand** and **niemand** are followed by **ander(e)s,** this is written with a small letter, e.g. **jemand/niemand ander(e)s.**

Continued

1 Ich habe es jemandem (*dat*) **gegeben**
I gave it to someone

Irgend jemand (*nom*) **hat es genommen**
Someone or other has stolen it

2 Er hat niemanden (*acc*) **gesehen**
He didn't see anyone

Er ist unterwegs niemandem (*dat*) **begegnet**
He encountered no-one on the way

3 Diese Aufgabe erfordert jemand Intelligentes
Someone intelligent is needed for this task

Indefinite Pronouns (contd)

keiner none

	MASC	SINGULAR FEM	NEUT	PLURAL ALL GENDERS
NOM	**keiner**	**keine**	**keins**	**keine**
ACC	**keinen**	**keine**	**keins**	**keine**
GEN	**keines**	**keiner**	**keines**	**keiner**
DAT	**keinem**	**keiner**	**keinem**	**keinen**

- It is declined like the article **kein, keine, kein** (see p 126) except in the nominative masculine and nominative and accusative neuter forms (→**1**)

- It may be used to refer to people or things (→**1**)

einer one

	MASC	SINGULAR FEM	NEUT
NOM	**einer**	**eine**	**ein(e)s**
ACC	**einen**	**eine**	**ein(e)s**
GEN	**eines**	**einer**	**eines**
DAT	**einem**	**einer**	**einem**

- This pronoun may be used to refer to either persons or things (→**2**)

- It exists only in the singular forms.

Continued

1 Keiner von ihnen hat es tuń können
Not one of them was able to do it

Gibst du mir eine Zigarette? — Tut mir leid, ich habe keine
Will you give me a cigarette? — Sorry, I haven't got any

2 Sie ist mit einem meiner Verwandten verlobt
She is engaged to one of my relatives

Wo sind die anderen Kinder? Ich sehe hier nur eins
Where are the rest of the children? I can only see one here

Gibst du mir einen? (e.g. **einen Whisky, einen Zehner** *etc*)
Gibst du mir eine? (e.g. **eine Zigarette, eine Blume** *etc*)
Gibst du mir eins? (e.g. **ein Buch, ein Butterbrot** *etc*)
Will you give me one?

Indefinite Pronouns (contd)

• Certain adjectives and articles can be used as pronouns.

• The following are all declined to agree in gender and number with the noun or pronoun they represent (→**1**):

mehrere several
ander other

derjenige that one
derselbe the same one

mancher some
jeder each (one), every one
jener that one
dieser this one
solcher such as that, such a one
mancher some, quite a few
einiger some
welcher which one
aller all
irgendwelcher someone or other; something or other
beide both
sämtliche all, the lot

• The following do not change whatever the gender or number of the noun or pronoun they represent (→**2**):

etwas some, something   **nichts** nothing, none
ein paar a few   **ein wenig** a little, a few
mehr more   **ein bißchen** a bit, a little

• When an adjective follows **etwas** or **nichts**, it takes a capital letter and declension endings: **etwas/nichts Gutes** something/nothing good.

1 Andere machen es besser (e.g. **Leute, Waschmaschinen** *etc*)
Others do it better

Mit einem solchen **kommst du nicht bis nach Hause** (e.g. **Wagen** *etc*)
You won't make it home in one like that

Alles, was er ihr schenkte, schickte sie sofort zurück
Everything that he gave her she sent back at once

Er war mit beiden **zufrieden** (e.g. **Computern, Autos** *etc*)
He was satisfied with both

2 Ich muß dir etwas **sagen**
I must tell you something

Etwas ist herausgefallen
Something fell out

Nichts ist geschehen
Nothing happened

Er ist mit nichts **zufrieden**
He is content with nothing

Gibst du mir bitte ein paar?
Will you give me a few?

Er hatte ein wenig **bei sich**
He had a little with him

Er braucht immer mehr, **um zu überleben**
He needs more and more to survive

Use of Adverbs

- Adverbs, or phrases which are used as adverbs, may:

  a) modify a verb (→**1**)

  b) modify an adjective (→**2**)

  c) modify another adverb (→**3**)

  d) modify a conjunction (→**4**)

  e) ask a question (→**5**)

  f) form verb prefixes (see p 72) (→**6**)

- Adverbs are also used, in much the same way as in English, to make the meaning of certain tenses more precise e.g.

  a) with continuous tenses (→**7**)

  b) to show a future meaning where the tense used is not future (→**8**)

Continued

1 Er ging langsam über die Brücke
He walked slowly over the bridge

2 Er ist ein ziemlich großer Kerl
He's quite a big chap

3 Sie arbeitet heute besonders tüchtig
She's working exceptionally well today

4 Wenn er es nur aufgeben wollte!
If only he would give it up!

5 Wann kommt er an?
When does he arrive?

6 falsch spielen to cheat (*at cards*)
hintragen to carry (*to a place*)

7 Er liest gerade die Zeitung
He's just reading the paper

8 Er wollte gerade aufstehen, als ...
He was just about to get up when ...

Wir fahren morgen nach Köln
We're driving to Cologne tomorrow

The Formation of Adverbs

- Many adverbs are simply adjectives used as adverbs. Used in this way, unlike adjectives, they are not declined (→**1**)

- Some adverbs are formed by adding **-weise** or **-sweise** to a noun (→**2**)

- Some adverbs are also formed by adding **-erweise** to an uninflected adjective.
  Such adverbs are used mainly to show the speaker's opinion (→**3**)

- There is also a class of adverbs which are not formed from other parts of speech e.g.
  unten, oben, leider (→**4**)
  and those shown in the paragraphs below.

- For the position of adverbs within a clause or sentence, see the section on sentence structure, pp 224 to 235.

- The following are some common adverbs of time:
  morgen tomorrow
  morgens in the mornings
  heute today
  endlich finally
  sofort at once
  immer always　　　　　　　　　　(→**5**)

- The following are some common adverbs of degree:
  äußerst extremely
  besonders especially
  ziemlich fairly
  beträchtlich considerably　　　　(→**6**)

Continued

1 **Habe ich das richtig gehört?**
Is it true what I've heard?

Sie war modern angezogen
She was fashionably dressed

2 **beispielsweise** for example
beziehungsweise or; or rather; that is to say
schrittweise step by step
zeitweise at times
zwangsweise compulsorily

3 **glücklicherweise** fortunately
komischerweise strangely enough
erstaunlicherweise astonishingly enough

4 **Unten wohnte Frau Schmidt**
Mrs Schmidt lived downstairs

Leider können wir nicht kommen
Unfortunately we cannot come

5 **Ich kann erst morgen kommen**
I can't come till tomorrow

Das Kind hat immer Hunger
The child is always hungry

6 **Das Paket war besonders schwer**
The parcel was unusually heavy

Diese Übung ist ziemlich leicht
This exercise is quite easy

Adverbs of place

In certain respects German adverbs of place behave very differently from their English counterparts:

- Where no movement, or movement within the same place, is involved, the adverb is used in its simple dictionary form (→**1**)

- Movement *away from the speaker* is shown by the presence of **hin** (→**2**)
  The following compound adverbs are therefore often used when movement away from the original position is concerned, even though a simple adverb would be used in English:

  wohin? where (to)?
  irgendwohin (to) somewhere or other
  überallhin everywhere
  dahin (to) there
  hierhin here
  dorthin there   (→**3**)

- Movement *towards the speaker* or central person is shown by the presence of **her**.
  The following compound adverbs are therefore often used to show movement towards a person:

  woher? where from?
  hierher here
  irgendwoher from somewhere or other
  daher from there
  überallher from all over   (→**4**)

Continued

1 Wo ist er? Where is he?
Er is nicht da He isn't there

Hier darf man nicht parken
You can't park here

2 Klaus und Ulli geben heute eine Party. Gehen wir hin?
Klaus and Ulli are giving a party today. Shall we go?

3 Wohin fährst du? Where are you going?

Sie liefen überallhin They ran everywhere

4 Woher kommst du? Where do you come from?

Woher hast du das? Where did you get that from?

Das habe ich irgendwoher gekriegt
I got that from somewhere or other

Comparison of Adverbs

- The **comparative** form of the adverb is obtained in exactly the same way as that of adjectives, i.e. by adding **-er** (→1)

- The **superlative** form is formed as follows:
                    am + *adverb* + **-sten/-esten**
  It is not declined (→2)

- Note the use of the comparative adverb with **immer** to show progression (→3)

- *the more ... the more ...* is expressed in German by **je ... desto ...** or **je ... um so ...** (→4)

- Some adverbial superlatives are used to show the extent of a quality rather than a comparison with others. These are as follows:
    spätestens at the latest
    höchstens at the most; at best
    wenigstens at least
    meistens mostly; most often
    strengstens strictly, absolutely
    bestens very well; very warmly   (→5)

- Two irregular comparatives and superlatives:
  gern → **lieber** → **am liebsten** (used with **haben**)
  well → better → best

  bald → **eher** → **am ehesten**
  soon → sooner → soonest   (→6)

1 **Er läuft schneller als seine Schwester**
  He runs faster than his sister

  Ich sehe ihn seltener als früher
  I see him less often than before

2 **Wer von ihnen arbeitet am schnellsten?**
  Which of them works fastest?

  Er ißt am meisten He eats most

3 **Die Mädchen sprachen immer lauter**
  The girls were talking more and more loudly

  Er fuhr immer langsamer
  He drove more and more slowly

4 **Je eher, desto besser** The sooner the better

5 **Er kommt meistens zu spät an**
  He usually arrives late

  Rauchen strengstens verboten!
  Smoking strictly prohibited

6 **Welches hast du am liebsten?**
  Which do you like best?

Emphasizers

These are words commonly used in German, as indeed in English, especially in the spoken language, to emphasize or modify in some way the meaning of the sentence. The following are some of the most common:

aber
Used to lend emphasis to a statement (→**1**)

denn
As well as its uses as a conjunction (see p 214), **denn** is widely used to emphasize the meaning. It often cannot be directly translated (→**2**)

doch
Is used as a positive reply in order to correct negative assumptions or impressions (→**3**)

It can strengthen an imperative (→**4**)

It can make a question out of a statement (→**5**)

mal
May be used with imperatives (→**6**)

It also has several idiomatic uses (→**7**)

ja
Strengthens a statement (→**8**)

It also has several idiomatic uses (→**9**)

schon
Is used familiarly with an imperative (→**10**)

It is also used in various idiomatic ways (→**11**)

1 **Das ist aber schön!** Oh that's pretty!
  Aber ja! Yes indeed!

2 **Was ist denn hier los?**
  What's going on here then?
  Wo denn? Where?

3 **Hat es dir nicht gefallen? — Doch!**
  Didn't you like it? — Oh yes, I did!

4 **Laß ihn doch!** Just leave him

5 **Das schaffst du doch?**
  You'll manage it, won't you?

6 **Komm mal her!** Come here!
  Moment mal! Just a minute!

7 **Mal sehen** We'll see
  Er soll es nur mal versuchen!
  Just let him try it!
  Hören Sie mal ... Look here now ...

8 **Er sieht ja wie seine Mutter aus**
  He looks like his mother
  Das kann ja sein That may well be

9 **Ja und?** So what?/What then?
  Das ist ja lächerlich That's ridiculous
  Das ist es ja That's just it

10 **Mach schon!** Get on with it!

11 **Wenn schon!** What of it?/So what?
  Schon gut Okay/Very well

Prepositions

In English, a preposition does not affect the word or phrase which it introduces e.g.

the women / a large meal / these events
with the women / *after* a large meal / *before* these events

In German, however, the noun following a preposition must be put in a certain *case*:   *accusative*   (→**1**)
dative   (→**2**)
genitive   (→**3**)

It is therefore important to learn each preposition with the case, or cases, it governs.

The following guidelines will help you:

- Prepositions which take the accusative or dative cases are much more common than those taking the genitive case.

- Certain prepositions may take a dative or accusative case, depending on whether *movement* is involved or not. This is explained further on pp 202 ff (→**4**)

- Prepositions are often used to complete the sense of certain verbs, as shown on p 76 ff (→**5**)

- After many prepositions, a shortened or *contracted* form of the definite article may be merged with the preposition to form one word, e.g.

auf + **das**	becomes **aufs**
bei + **dem**	becomes **beim**
zu + **der**	becomes **zur**

Continued

1 **Es ist für dich**
   It's for you
   Wir sind durch die ganze Welt gereist
   We travelled all over the world

2 **Er ist mit seiner Frau gekommen**
   He came with his wife

3 **Es ist ihm trotz seiner Bemühungen nicht gelungen**
   Despite his efforts, he still didn't succeed

4 **Es liegt auf dem Tisch**
   It's on the table (*dative*: no movement implied)
   Lege es bitte auf den Tisch Please put it on the table
   (*accusative*: movement *onto* the table)

5 **Ich warte auf meinen Mann**
   I'm waiting for my husband

Prepositions: contracted forms (contd)

Such contractions are possible with the following prepositions:

preposition	+ **das**	+ **den**	+ **dem**	+ **der**
hinter	hinters*	hintern*	hinterm*	
über	übers*	übern*	überm*	
unter	unters*	untern*	unterm*	
zu			zum	zur
an	ans		am	
vor	vors*		vorm*	
in	ins		im	
bei			beim	
von			vom	
durch	durchs*			
für	fürs*			
auf	aufs*			
um	ums*			

- Those forms marked with an asterisk are suitable only for use in colloquial, spoken German.
  All other forms (not marked with an asterisk) may be safely used in any context, formal or informal (→**1**)

- Contracted forms are obviously not used where the article is to be stressed (→**2**)

- Other contracted forms involving prepositions, as shown on pp 164 and 174, occur:
  1) in the introduction to relative clauses (→**3**)
  2) with personal pronouns representing inanimate objects (→**4**)

Continued

1 **Wir gehen heute Abend ins Theater**
We are going to the theatre this evening

Er geht zur Schule
He goes to school

Das kommt vom Trinken
That comes from drinking

2 **In dem Anzug kann ich mich nicht sehen lassen!**
I can't go out in that suit!

3 **Die Bank, worauf wir saßen, war etwas wackelig**
The bench we were sitting on was rather wobbly

4 **Er war damit zufrieden**
He was satisfied with that

Er hat es darauf gesetzt
He put it on it

Prepositions followed by the Dative Case

Some of the most common prepositions taking the dative case are:

aus	gegenüber	seit
außer	mit	von
bei	nach	zu

aus
- as a preposition meaning *out of/from* (→**1**)
- as a separable verbal prefix (see p 72) (→**2**)

außer
- as a preposition meaning: *out of*   (→**3**)
  except   (→**4**)

bei
- as a preposition meaning: *at the home/shop/work (etc) of* (→**5**)
  near (→**6**)
  in the course of/during (→**7**)
- as a separable verbal prefix (see p 72) (→**8**)

gegenüber
- as a preposition meaning: *opposite* (→**9**)
  to(wards) (→**10**)
  - *NOTE*:   when used as a preposition, **gegenüber** is placed *after a pronoun*, but may be placed *before or after a noun*
- as a separable verbal prefix (→**11**)

Continued

1 **Er trinkt aus der Flasche**
He is drinking out of the bottle
Er kommt aus Essen He comes from Essen

2 **aushalten** to endure →
Ich halte es nicht mehr aus
I can't stand it any longer

3 **außer Gefahr/Betrieb** out of danger/order

4 **alle außer mir** all except me

5 **Bei uns in Schottland**
At home in Scotland
Er wohnt immer noch bei seinen Eltern
He still lives with his parents

6 **Er saß bei mir**
He was sitting next to me

7 **Ich singe immer beim Arbeiten**
I always sing when I'm working
Bei unserer Ankunft ...
On our arrival ...

8 **Er stand seinem Freund bei**
He stood by his friend

9 **Er wohnt uns gegenüber**
He lives opposite us

10 **Er ist mir gegenüber immer sehr freundlich gewesen**
He has always been very friendly towards me

11 **gegenüberstehen** to face/to have an attitude towards →
Er steht ihnen kritisch gegenüber
He takes a critical view of them

Prepositions followed by the Dative Case
(contd)

mit
- as a preposition meaning *with* (→**1**)
- as a separable verbal prefix (see p 72) (→**2**)

nach
- as a preposition meaning: *after* (→**3**)
                              to (→**4**)
                              according to (it can be placed after
  the noun with this meaning) (→**5**)
- as a separable verbal prefix (see p 72) (→**6**)

seit
- as a preposition meaning: *since* (→**7**)
                                for (of time; note the tense!) (→**8**)

von
- as a preposition meaning: *from* (→**9**)
                                 about (→**10**)
- as an alternative, often preferred, to the genitive case (→**11**)
- meaning *by*, to introduce the agent of a passive action (see p 34)
  (→**12**)

zu
- as a preposition meaning: *to* (→**13**)
                                 for (→**14**)
- as a separable verbal prefix (see p 72) (→**15**)

Continued

1 **Er ging mit seinen Freunden spazieren**
He went walking with his friends

2 **jemanden mitnehmen** to give someone a lift →
Nimmst du mich bitte mit?
Will you give me a lift please?

3 **Nach zwei Stunden kam er wieder**
He returned two hours later

4 **Er ist nach London gereist**
He went to London

5 **Ihrer Sprache nach ist sie Süddeutsche**
From the way she spoke I would say she is from southern Germany

6 **nachmachen** to copy →
Sie macht mir alles nach
She copies everything I do

7 **Seit der Zeit ...**
Since then ...

8 **Ich wohne seit zwei Jahren in Frankfurt**
I've been living in Frankfurt for two years

9 **Von Frankfurt sind wir weiter nach München gefahren**
From Frankfurt we went on to Munich

10 **Ich weiß nichts von ihm**
I know nothing about him

11 **Die Mutter von diesen Mädchen ...**
The mother of these girls ...
Sie ist eine Freundin von Horst
She is a friend of Horst's

12 **Er ist von unseren Argumenten überzeugt worden**
He was convinced by our arguments

13 **Er ging zum Arzt**
He went to the doctor's

14 **Wir sind zum Essen eingeladen**
We're invited for dinner

15 **zumachen** to shut →
Mach die Tür zu
Shut the door

Prepositions followed by the Accusative Case

The most common of these are:

durch   für   ohne   wider
entlang   gegen   um

durch

- as a preposition meaning *through* (→**1**)
- preceding the inanimate agent of a passive action (see p 34) (→**2**)
- as a separable verbal prefix

entlang

- as a preposition meaning *along*, in which case it follows the noun (→**3**)
- as a separable verbal prefix (→**4**)

für

- as a preposition meaning: *for*   (→**5**)
                              to   (→**6**)
- in **was für/was für ein** *what kind of/what*, as shown on p 144 and p 180 (→**7**)

gegen

- as a preposition meaning: *against* (→**8**)
                                  towards/getting on for (→**9**)
- as a separable verbal prefix

Continued

1 **durch das Fenster blicken**
  to look through the window

2 **Durch seine Bemühungen wurden alle gerettet**
  Everyone was saved through his efforts

3 **die Straße entlang**
  along the street

4 **Wir gingen die Straße entlang**
  We went along the street

5 **Ich habe es für dich getan**
  I did it for you

6 **Das ist für ihn sehr wichtig**
  That is very important to him

7 **Was für Äpfel sind das?**
  What kind of apples are they?

8 **Stelle es gegen die Mauer**
  Put it against the wall
  Haben Sie ein Mittel gegen Schnupfen?
  Have you something for (= against) colds?
  Ich habe nichts dagegen
  I've got nothing against it

9 **Wir sind gegen vier angekommen**
  We arrived at getting on for/around four o'clock

Prepositions followed by the Accusative Case (contd)

ohne

- as a preposition meaning *without* (→**1**)

um

- as a preposition meaning: *(a)round/round about* (→**2**)
  at (in time expressions) (→**3**)
  for (after certain verbs) (→**4**)
  about (after certain verbs) (→**5**)
  by (in expressions of quantity) (→**6**)
- as a variable verbal prefix (see p 74) (→**7**)

wider

- as a preposition meaning *contrary to/against* (→**8**)
- as a variable verbal prefix (see p 74) (→**9**)

Continued

1 **Ohne ihn geht's nicht**
It won't work without him

2 **um die Ecke** (a)round the corner

3 **Es fängt um neun Uhr an** It begins at nine

4 **Sie baten ihre Mutter um Kekse**
They asked their mother for some biscuits

5 **Es handelt sich um dein Benehmen**
It's a question of your behaviour

6 **Es ist um zehn Mark billiger**
It is cheaper by ten marks

7 **umarmen** to embrace (*inseparable*) →
Er hat sie umarmt
He gave her a hug

   umfallen to fall over (*separable*) →
Er ist umgefallen
He fell over

8 **Das geht mir wider die Natur**
That's against my nature

9 **widersprechen** to go against (*inseparable*) →
Das hat meinen Wünschen widersprochen
That went against my wishes

   (sich) widerspiegeln to reflect (*separable*) →
Der Baum spiegelt sich im Wasser wider
The tree is reflected in the water

Prepositions followed by the Dative or the Accusative

These prepositions are followed by:
the **accusative** when *movement towards* a different place is
involved
the **dative** when *position* is described as opposed to movement,
or when the movement is *within* the same place.

- The most common prepositions in this category are:

  in *in/into/to* (→**1**)
  an *on/at/to*
  auf *on/in/to/at*
  unter *under/among* (→**2**)
  über *over/across/above*
  vor *in front of/before*
  hinter *behind*
  neben *next to/beside*
  zwischen *between* (→**3**)

- These prepositions may also be used with figurative meanings as
  part of a *verb + preposition* construction (see p 76).
  The case following **auf** or **an** is then not the same after all verbs
  (→**4**)
  It is therefore best to learn such constructions together with the
  case which follows them.

- Many of these prepositions are also used as verb prefixes in the
  same way as the prepositions described on pp 202 to 209 (→**5**)

Continued

1 Er ging ins Zimmer (*acc*)
He entered the room

Im Zimmer (*dat*) **warteten viele Leute auf ihn**
A lot of people were waiting for him in the room

2 Er stellte sich unter den Baum (*acc*)
He (came and) stood under the tree

Er lebte dort unter Freunden (*dat*)
There he lived among friends

3 Er legte es zwischen die beiden Teller (*acc*)
He put it between the two plates

Das Dorf liegt zwischen den Bergen (*dat*)
The village lies between the mountains

4 sich verlassen auf (+ *acc*) to depend on
bestehen auf (+ *dat*) to insist on

glauben an (+ *acc*) to believe in
leiden an (+ *dat*) to suffer from

5 anrechnen to charge for (*separable*) →
Das wird Ihnen später angerechnet
You'll be charged for that later

aufsetzen to put on (*separable*) →
Sie setzte sich den Hut auf
She put her hat on

überqueren to cross (*inseparable*) →
Sie hat die Straße überquert
She crossed the street

Prepositions followed by the Genitive Case

The following are some of the more common prepositions which take the genitive case:

diesseits *on this side of*
jenseits *on the other side of* (→**1**)
beiderseits *on both sides of*
innerhalb *within/inside* (→**2**)
außerhalb *outside*
während* *during* (→**3**)
statt* *instead of*
trotz* *in spite of* (→**4**)
wegen* *on account of* (→**5**)
infolge *as a result of*
hinsichtlich *with regard to*
... halber *for ... sake/because of ...*
um ... willen *for ... sake/because of ...*

- Those prepositions marked with an asterisk may also be followed by the dative case (→**6**)

- Note that special forms of the possessive and relative pronouns are used with **wegen, halber** and **willen** (→**7**)

1 **jenseits der Grenze**
  on the other side of the frontier

2 **innerhalb dieses Zeitraums**
  within this period of time

3 **während der Vorstellung**
  during the performance

4 **trotz seiner Befürchtungen**
  despite his fears

5 **wegen der neuen Stelle**
  because of the new job

6 **trotz allem** in spite of everything
  wegen mir because of me

7 **meinetwegen** on my account, because of me
  deinetwegen on your account, because of you
  seinetwegen on his account, because of him
  ihretwegen on her/their account, because of her/them
  unsertwegen on our account, because of us
  euertwegen on your account, because of you
  Ihretwegen on your account, because of you (*polite*)
  derentwegen for whose sake, for her/their/its sake
  dessentwegen for whose sake, for his/its sake

  meinethalben *etc* on my *etc* account
  derenthalben on whose account, on her/their/its account
  dessenthalben on whose account, on his/its account

  meinetwillen *etc* for my *etc* sake
  derentwillen for whose sake, for her/its/their sake
  dessentwillen for whose sake, for his/its sake

Co-ordinating Conjunctions

These are used to link words, phrases or clauses (→**1**)

- These are the main co-ordinating conjunctions:

und	and (→**1**)
oder	or (→**2**)
aber	but (→**3**)
	however (→**4**)
denn	for (→**5**)
sondern	but (after a negative construction) (→**6**)

- These do not cause subject-verb inversion, i.e. the verb follows the subject in the normal way (see p 224) (→**1-6**)

- Inversion may however be caused by something other than the co-ordinating conjunction, e.g. **dann, trotzdem, montags** in the examples opposite (→**7**)

- When used with the meaning of *however*, **aber** is placed within the clause, and not at the beginning (→**4**)

- When linked by co-ordinating conjunctions, no comma is required between clauses (cf p 240).

Continued

1 **Horst und Veronika** Horst and Veronika
   Er ging in die Stadt und kaufte sich ein neues Hemd
   He went into town and bought himself a new shirt

2 **Er hatte noch nie Whisky oder Schnaps getrunken**
   He had never drunk whisky or schnapps
   Willst du eins, oder hast du vielleicht keinen Hunger?
   Do you want one or aren't you hungry?

3 **Wir wollten ins Kino, aber wir hatten kein Geld**
   We wanted to go to the cinema but we had no money

4 **Ich wollte ins Theater; er aber wollte nicht mit**
   I wanted to go the theatre; however he wouldn't come

5 **Wir wollten heute fahren, denn montags ist weniger Verkehr**
   We wanted to travel today because the traffic is lighter on Mondays

6 **Er ist nicht alt, sondern jung**
   He isn't old, but young

7 **Er hat sie besucht, und dann ist er wieder nach Hause gegangen**
   He paid her a visit and then went home again
   Wir wollten doch ins Kino, aber trotzdem sind wir zu Hause geblieben
   We wanted to go to the cinema, but even so we stayed at home
   Wir wollten heute fahren, denn montags ist der Verkehr geringer
   We wanted to travel today because there is less traffic on Mondays

Double Co-ordinating Conjunctions

These conjunctions consist of two separate elements, like their English counterparts e.g.

not only ... but also ...

The following are widely used:

sowohl ... als (auch) *both ... and*

- This may link words or phrases (→**1**)

- The verb is usually plural, whether the subjects are singular or plural (→**1**)

weder ... noch *neither ... nor*

- This may link words or phrases (→**2**)

- It may also link clauses, and inversion of subject and verb then takes place in both clauses (→**3**)

- The verb is plural unless both subjects are singular (→**4**)

Continued

1 **Sowohl sein Vater als auch seine Mutter haben sich darüber gefreut**
   Both his father and his mother were pleased about it
   Sowohl unser Lehrkörper als auch unsere Schüler haben teilgenommen
   Both our staff and our pupils took part

2 **Weder Georg noch sein Bruder kannte das Mädchen**
   Neither Georg nor his brother knew the girl

3 **Weder mag ich ihn, noch respektiere ich ihn**
   I neither like nor respect him

4 **Weder die Befürworter noch die Gegner haben recht**
   Neither the supporters nor the opponents are right
   Weder du noch ich würde es schaffen
   Neither you nor I would be able to do it

Double Co-ordinating Conjunctions (contd)

nicht nur ... sondern auch *not only ... but also*

- This is used to link clauses as well as words and phrases (→**1**)

- The word order is: inversion of subject and verb in the first clause, and normal order in the second (→**2**)
  However, if **nicht nur** does not begin the clause, normal order prevails (→**3**)

- The verb agrees in number with the subject nearest to it (→**4**)

entweder ... oder *either ... or*

- The verb agrees with the subject nearest it (→**5**)

- The normal word order is: inversion in the first clause, and normal order in the second (→**6**)
  However, it is possible to use normal order in the first clause, and this may lend a more threatening tone to the statement (→**7**)

teils ... teils *partly ... partly*

- The verb is normally plural unless both subjects are singular (→**8**)

- Inversion of subject and verb takes place in both clauses (→**9**)

1 **Er ist nicht nur geschickt, sondern auch intelligent**
Nicht nur ist er geschickt, sondern er ist auch intelligent
He is not only skilful but also intelligent

2 **Nicht nur hat es die ganze Zeit geregnet, sondern ich habe mir auch noch das Bein gebrochen**
Not only did it rain the whole time, but I also broke my leg

3 **Es hat nicht nur die ganze Zeit geregnet, sondern ich habe mir auch noch das Bein gebrochen**
Not only did it rain the whole time, but I also broke my leg

4 **Nicht nur ich, sondern auch die Mädchen sind dafür verantwortlich**
Not just me, but the girls too are responsible
Nicht nur sie, sondern auch ich habe es gehört
It wasn't only they who heard it — I heard it too

5 **Entweder du oder Georg muß es getan haben**
It must have been either you or Georg who did it

6 **Entweder komme ich morgen vorbei, oder ich rufe dich an**
I'll either drop in tomorrow or I'll give you a ring

7 **Entweder du gibst das sofort auf, oder du kriegst kein Taschengeld mehr**
Either you give it up immediately, or you get no more pocket money

8 **Die Studenten waren teils Deutsche, teils Ausländer**
The students were partly German and partly from abroad

9 **Teils bin ich überzeugt, teils bleibe ich skeptisch**
A bit of me is convinced, and a bit remains sceptical

Subordinating Conjunctions

These are used to link clauses in such a way as to make one clause dependent on another for its meaning. The dependent clause is called a **subordinate clause** and the other a **main clause**.

- The subordinate clause is always separated from the rest of the sentence by commas (→**1**)

- The subordinate clause may precede the main clause. When this happens, the verb and subject of the main clause are inverted, i.e. they swap places, as shown as p 226 (→**2**)

- The finite part of the verb (i.e. the conjugated part) is always at the end of a subordinate clause (see p 228) (→**3**)

- For compound tenses in subordinate clauses, it is the **auxiliary** (the main part of the verb) which comes last, after the participle or infinitive used to form the compound tense (see the section on compound tenses) (→**4**)

- Any **modal verb** (**mögen, können** etc — p 52 ff) used in a subordinate clause is placed last in the clause (→**5**)

  EXCEPTION: when the modal verb is in a compound tense, the order is as shown (→**6**)

Continued

     MAIN CLAUSE   *SUBORDINATE CLAUSE*

1 **Er ist zu Fuß gekommen, weil der Bus zu teuer ist**
  He came on foot because the bus is too dear
  Ich trinke viel Bier, obwohl es nicht gesund ist
  I drink a lot of beer although it isn't good for me
  Wir haben weiter gefeiert, nachdem sie gegangen waren
  We carried on the party after they went

    SUBORDINATE CLAUSE   *MAIN CLAUSE*

2 **Weil der Bus zu teuer ist, geht er zu Fuß**
  Obwohl es nicht gesund ist, trinke ich viel Bier
  Nachdem sie gegangen waren, haben wir weiter gefeiert

3 **Als er uns sah, ist er davongelaufen**
  Er ist davongelaufen, als er uns sah
  He ran away when he saw us

4 **Nachdem er gegessen hatte, ging er hinaus**
  He went out after he had eaten

5 **Da er nicht mit uns sprechen wollte, ist er davongelaufen**
  Since he didn't want to speak to us he ran away

6 **Da er nicht mit uns hat sprechen wollen, ist er davongelaufen**
  Since he didn't want to speak to us, he ran away

Subordinating conjunctions (contd)

- Here are some common examples of subordinating conjunctions and their uses:

  nachdem after (→**1**)
  indem while
  wenn when/whenever; if (→**2**)
  als when (→**3**)
  wann when (*interrogative*) (→**4**)
  während while (→**5**)
  bevor before
  sobald as soon as
  wohin to where
  worin in which
  inwiefern to what extent
  soweit as far as
  worauf whereupon; on which
  als ob as if/as though
  weil because (→**6**)
  seitdem since
  bis until (→**7**)
  wo where
  wie as/like
  da as/since (→**8**)
  obwohl although
  damit so (that)
  so daß such that, so that
  ob whether, if

Continued

1 **Er wird uns Bescheid sagen können, nachdem er angerufen hat**
  Nachdem er angerufen hat, wird er uns Bescheid sagen können
  He will be able to let us know for certain, once he has phoned

2 **Wenn ich ins Kino gehe ...**
  When(ever) I go to the cinema ...
  Ich komme, wenn du willst
  I'll come if you like

3 **Es regnete, als ich in Köln ankam**
  Als ich in Köln ankam, regnete es
  It was raining when I arrived in Cologne

4 **Er möchte wissen, wann der Zug ankommt**
  He would like to know when the train is due to arrive

5 **Während seine Frau die Koffer auspackte, machte er das Abendessen**
  Er machte das Abendessen, während seine Frau die Koffer auspackte
  He made the supper while his wife unpacked the cases

6 **Wir haben den Hund nicht mitgenommen, weil im Auto nicht genug Platz war**
  Weil im Auto nicht genug Platz war, haben wir den Hund nicht mitgenommen
  We didn't take the dog because there wasn't enough room in the car

7 **Ich warte, bis du zurückkommst**
  I'll wait till you get back

8 **Da er nicht kommen wollte, ...**
  Since he didn't want to come ...

Word Order: Main Clauses

- In a main clause the subject comes first and is followed by the verb, as in English:

  His mother (*subject*) drinks (*verb*) whisky (→**1**)

- If the verb is in a compound or passive tense, the auxiliary follows the subject and the past participle or infinitive goes to the end of the clause (→**2**)

- The verb is the second concept in a main clause. The first concept may be a word, phrase or clause (→**3**)

- Any reflexive pronoun *follows* the main verb in simple tenses and the auxiliary in compound tenses (→**4**)

- The order for articles, adjectives and nouns is as in English: "a/the/this/that" + *adjective(s)* + *noun* (→**5**)

- A direct object usually follows an indirect, except where the direct object is a personal pronoun.
  But the indirect object can be placed last for emphasis, providing it is not a pronoun (→**6**)

- The position of adverbial expressions (see p 188) is not fixed. As a general rule they are placed close to the words to which they refer. Adverbial items of *time* often come first in the clause, but this is flexible (→**7**)
  Adverbials of *place* can be placed at the beginning of a clause when emphasis is required (→**8**)
  Adverbial items of *manner* are more likely to be within the clause, close to the word to which they refer (→**9**)

- Where there is more than one adverb, a useful rule of thumb is "time, manner, place" (→**10**)

Continued

1 Seine Mutter trinkt Whisky
His mother drinks whisky

2 Sie wird dir etwas sagen She will tell you something
Sie hat mir nichts gesagt She told me nothing
Es ist für ihn gekauft worden It was bought for him

        1   2
3 Die neuen Waren   **kommen**   **morgen**
The new goods   are coming   tomorrow
          1   2
Was du gesagt hast, stimmt nicht
What you said   isn't true

4 Er rasierte sich He shaved
Er hat sich rasiert He (has) shaved

5 ein alter Mann an old man
diese alten Sachen these old things

6 Ich gab dem Mann das Geld I gave the man the money
Ich gab ihm das Geld I gave him the money
Ich gab es ihm I gave him it/I gave it to him
Ich gab es dem Mann I gave it to the man
Er gab das Geld seiner Schwester
He gave the money to his sister (*not his brother*)

7 Gestern gingen wir ins Theater } We went to the theatre
Wir gingen gestern ins Theater }   yesterday

8 Dort haben sie Fußball gespielt } They played football
Sie haben dort Fußball gespielt }   there

9 Sie spielen gut Fußball They play football well
Das war furchtbar teuer It was terribly expensive

10 Wir haben gestern gut hierhin gefunden
We found our way here all right yesterday

Word Order: Main Clauses (contd)

- A pronoun object precedes all adverbs (→**1**)
- While the main verb must normally remain the second concept, the first concept need not always be the subject. Main clauses can begin with many things, including:

    an adverb (→**2**)
    a direct or indirect object (→**3**)
    an infinitive phrase (→**4**)
    a complement (→**5**)
    a past participle (→**6**)
    a prepositional phrase (→**7**)
    a clause acting as the object of the verb (→**8**)
    a subordinate clause (→**9**)

- If the subject does not begin a main clause, the verb and subject must be turned around or "inverted" (→**2-9**)
- Beginning a sentence with something other than the subject is frequent in German.

    It may however also be used for special effect to:
    highlight whatever is placed first in the clause (→**10**)
    emphasize the subject of the clause by forcing it from its initial position to the end of the clause (→**11**)

- After inversion, any reflexive pronoun precedes the subject, unless the subject is a pronoun (→**12**)
- The following do not cause inversion when placed at the beginning of a main clause, although inversion may be caused by something else placed after them:

    und, allein, oder, sondern, denn (→**13**)
    ja and **nein** (→**14**)
    certain exclamations: **ach, also, nun** *etc* (→**15**)
    words or phrases qualifying the subject: **nur, sogar, auch** *etc* (→**16**)

1 **Sie haben es gestern sehr billig gekauft**
They bought it very cheaply yesterday

2 **Gestern sind wir ins Theater gegangen**
We went to the theatre yesterday

3 **So ein Kind habe ich noch nie gesehen!**
I've never seen such a child!
Seinen Freunden wollte er es nicht zeigen
He wouldn't show it to his friends

4 **Seinen Freunden zu helfen, hat er nicht versucht**
He didn't try to help his friends

5 **Deine Schwester war es** It was your sister

6 **Geraucht hatte er nie** He had never smoked

7 **In diesem Haus ist Mozart auf die Welt gekommen**
Mozart was born in this house

8 **Was mit ihm los war, haben wir nicht herausgefunden**
We never discovered what was wrong with him

9 **Nachdem ich ihn gesehen hatte, ging ich nach Hause**
I went home after seeing him

10 **Dem würde ich nichts sagen!** I wouldn't tell *him* anything

11 **An der Ecke stand eine riesengroße Fabrik**
A huge factory stood on the corner

12 **Daran erinnerten sich die Zeugen nicht**
The witnesses didn't remember that
Daran erinnerten sie sich nicht They didn't remember that

13 **Peter ging nach Hause, und Elsa blieb auf der Party**
Peter went home and Elsa stayed at the party
BUT   **Peter ging nach Hause, und unterwegs sah er Kurt**
          Peter went home and on the way he saw Kurt

14 **Nein, ich will nicht** No, I don't want to
BUT   **Nein, das tue ich nicht** No I won't do that

15 **Also, wir fahren nach Hamburg** So we'll go to Hamburg
BUT   **Also, nach Hamburg wollt ihr fahren**
          So you want to go to Hamburg

16 **Sogar seine Mutter wollte es ihm nicht glauben**
Even his mother wouldn't believe him
BUT   **Sogar mit dem Zug ginge es nicht schneller**
          It would be no faster even by train

Word Order: Subordinate Clauses

- A subordinate clause may be introduced by:
  a relative pronoun (see p 174) (→**1**)
  a subordinating conjunction (see p 222) (→**2-3**)

- The subject follows the opening conjunction or relative pronoun
  — **wir** and **er** in examples **1-3**

- The main verb almost always goes to the end of a subordinate
  clause (→**1-3**)

  The exceptions to this are:

  1. in a **wenn** clause where **wenn** is omitted (see p 64) (→**4**)
  2. in an indirect statement without **daß** (see p 64) (→**5**)

- The order for articles, nouns, adjectives, adverbs, direct and
  indirect objects is the same as for main clauses (see
  p 224), but they are all placed between the subject of the clause
  and the verb (→**6**)

- If the subject of a reflexive verb in a subordinate clause is a
  pronoun, the order is *subject pronoun* + *reflexive pronoun*
  (→**7**) If the subject is a noun, the reflexive pronoun may follow
  or precede it (→**8**)

- Where one subordinate clause lies inside another, both still obey
  the order rule for subordinate clauses (→**9**)

1 Die Kinder, die wir gesehen haben ...
The children whom we saw ...

2 Da er nicht schwimmen wollte, ist er nicht mitgekommen
As he didn't want to swim he didn't come

3 Ich weiß, daß er zur Zeit in London wohnt
I know he's living in London at the moment
Ich weiß nicht, ob er kommt
I don't know if he's coming

4 Findest du meine Uhr, so ruf mich bitte an
(= Wenn du meine Uhr findest, ruf mich bitte an)
If you find my watch, please give me a ring

5 Er meint, er werde es innerhalb einer Stunde schaffen
(= Er meint, daß er es innerhalb einer Stunde schaffen werde)
He thinks (that) he would manage it inside an hour

6 *main clause:*
Er ist gestern mit seiner Mutter in die Stadt gefahren
He went to town with his mother yesterday
subordinate clauses:
Da er gestern mit seiner Mutter in die Stadt gefahren ist ...
Since he went to town with his mother yesterday ...
Der Junge, der gestern mit seiner Mutter in die Stadt gefahren ist ...
The boy who went to town with his mother yesterday ...
Ich weiß, daß er gestern mit seiner Mutter in die Stadt gefahren ist
I know that he went to town with his mother yesterday

7 Weil er sich nicht setzen wollte ...
Because he wouldn't sit down ...

8 Weil das Kind sich nicht setzen wollte, ...
OR   **Weil sich das Kind nicht setzen wollte, ...**
          Because the child wouldn't sit down ...

9 Er wußte, daß der Mann, mit dem er gesprochen hatte, bei einer Baufirma arbeitete
He knew that the man he had been speaking to worked for a construction company

Word Order (contd)

In the Imperative

- normal order (→**1**)

- with reflexive verbs (→**2**)

- with separable verbs (→**3**)

- with separable reflexive verbs (→**4**)

In Direct and Indirect speech

- the verb of saying ("he replied/he said") must be inverted if it is placed within a quotation (→**5**)

- the position of the verb in indirect speech depends on whether or not **daß** (see p 66) is used (→**6**)

Verbs with Separable Prefixes (see pp 72 to 75)

- in main clauses the verb and prefix are separated in simple tenses and imperative forms (→**7**)

- for compound tenses of main clauses and all tenses of subordinate clauses, the verb and its prefix are united at the end of the clause (→**8**)

- in a present infinitive phrase (see p 46), the verb and prefix are joined together by **zu** and placed at the end of the phrase (→**9**)

1 **Hol mir das Buch!** (*singular*)
  Holt mir das Buch! (*plural*)   } Fetch me that book!
  Holen Sie mir das Buch! (*polite*)

2 **Wasch dich sofort!** Wash yourself at once!
  Wascht euch sofort! Wash yourselves at once!
  Waschen Sie sich sofort! (*polite*)

3 **Hör jetzt auf!** (*singular*)
  Hört jetzt auf! (*plural*)   } Stop it!
  Hören Sie jetzt auf! (*polite*)

4 **Dreh dich um!** (*singular*)
  Dreht euch um! (*plural*)   } Turn round!
  Drehen Sie sich um! (*polite*)

5 **"Meine Mutter" sagte er, "kommt erst morgen an"**
  "My mother", he said, "won't arrive till tomorrow"

6 **Er sagte, daß sie erst am nächsten Tag ankomme**
  He said that she would not arrive until the next day
  Er sagte, sie komme erst am nächsten Tag an
  He said she would not arrive until the next day

7 **Er machte die Tür zu** He closed the door
  Ich räume zuerst auf I'll clean up first
  Hol mich um 7 ab! Pick me up at 7 o'clock!

8 **Er hat die Tür zugemacht** He closed the door
  Ich werde zuerst aufräumen I'll clean up first
  Er wurde um 7 abgeholt He was picked up at 7
  Wenn du mich um 7 abholst, ... If you pick me up at 7 ...
  Nachdem du mich abgeholt hast, ...
  After you've picked me up ...

9 **Um frühzeitig anzukommen, fuhren wir sofort ab**
  In order to arrive early we left immediately

Question Forms

Direct Questions

- In German, a direct question is formed by simply inverting the verb and subject (→**1**)

- In compound tenses (see pp 22 ff), the past participle or infinitive goes to the end of the clause (→**2**)

- A statement can be made into a question by the addition of **nicht, nicht wahr** or **doch**, as with "isn't it" in English (→**3**)
  Questions formed in this way normally expect the answer to be "yes".

- When a question is put in the negative, **doch** can be used to answer it more positively than **ja** (→**4**)

Questions Formed Using Interrogative Words

- When questions are formed with **interrogative adverbs**, the subject and verb are inverted (→**5**)

- When questions are formed with **interrogative pronouns** and **adjectives** (see pp 144 and 176 to 178), the word order is that of direct statements:
  1. as the subject of the verb at the beginning of the clause they do not cause inversion (→**6**)
  2. if *not* the subject of the verb *and* at the beginning of the clause they do cause inversion (→**7**)

Indirect Questions

These are questions following verbs of asking and wondering etc. The verb comes at the end of an indirect question (→**8**)

1 Magst du ihn?
Do you like him?
Gehst du ins Kino?
Do you go to the cinema? Are you going to the cinema?

2 Hast du ihn gesehen?
Did you see him? Have you seen him?
Wird sie mit ihm kommen?
Will she come with him?

3 Das stimmt, nicht (wahr)? That's true, isn't it?
Das schaffst du doch? You'll manage, won't you?

4 Glaubst du mir nicht? — Doch!
Don't you believe me? — Yes I do!

5 Wann ist er gekommen? When did he come?
Wo willst du hin? Where are you off to?

6 Wer hat das gemacht? Who did this?

7 Wem hast du es geschenkt? Who did you give it to?

8 Er fragte, ob du mitkommen wolltest
He asked if you wanted to come
Er möchte wissen, warum du nicht gekommen bist
He would like to know why you didn't come

Negatives

A statement or question is made negative by adding:

nicht (*not*) or **nie** (*never*)

- The negative may be placed next to the phrase or word to which it refers. The negative meaning can be shifted from one element of the sentence to another in this way (→**1**)

- **nie** can be placed at the beginning of a sentence for added emphasis, in which case subject-verb inversion occurs (→**2**)

- **nicht** comes at the end of a negative imperative, except when the verb is separable, in which case **nicht** *precedes* the separable prefix (→**3**)

- The combination **nicht ein** is usually replaced by forms of **kein** (see p 126) (→**4**)

- **doch** (see p 196) is used in place of **ja** to contradict a negative statement (→**5**)

- Negative comparison is made with **nicht ... sondern** (*not ... but*). This construction is used to correct a previous false impression or idea (→**6**)

1 **Mit ihr wollte er nicht sprechen**
He didn't want to speak to *her*
Er wollte nicht mit ihr sprechen
He didn't *want* to speak to her

Er will nicht morgen nach Hause
OR **Morgen will er nicht nach Hause**
He doesn't want to go home *tomorrow*
Er will morgen nicht nach Hause
He doesn't want to go *home* tomorrow

Wohnen Sie nicht in Dortmund?
Don't you live in Dortmund?
Warum ist er nicht mitgekommen?
Why didn't he come with you?
Waren Sie nie in Dortmund?
Have you never been to Dortmund?

2 **Nie war sie glücklicher gewesen**
She had never been happier

3 **Iß das nicht!** Don't eat that!
Beeilen Sie sich nicht! Don't hurry!
BUT **Geh nicht weg!** Don't go away!

4 **Gibt es keine Plätzchen?** Aren't there any biscuits?
Kein einziges Kind hatte die Arbeit geschrieben
Not a single child had done the work

5 **Du kommst nicht mit — Doch, ich komme mit**
You're not coming — Yes I am

6 **Nicht Joachim, sondern sein Bruder war es**
It wasn't Joachim, but his brother

Numbers

Cardinal (*one, two etc*)		**Ordinal** (*first, second etc*)	
null	0		
eins	1	**der erste**[2]	1.
zwei[1]	2	**der zweite**[1]	2.
drei	3	**der dritte**	3.
vier	4	**der vierte**	4.
fünf	5	**der fünfte**	5.
sechs	6	**der sechste**	6.
sieben	7	**der siebte**	7.
acht	8	**der achte**	8.
neun	9	**der neunte**	9.
zehn	10	**der zehnte**	10.
elf	11	**der elfte**	11.
zwölf	12	**der zwölfte**	12.
dreizehn	13	**der dreizehnte**	13.
vierzehn	14	**der vierzehnte**	14.
fünfzehn	15	**der fünfzehnte**	15.
sechzehn	16	**der sechzehnte**	16.
siebzehn	17	**der siebzehnte**	17.
achtzehn	18	**der achtzehnte**	18.
neunzehn	19	**der neunzehnte**	19.
zwanzig	20	**der zwanzigste**	20.
einundzwanzig	21	**der einundzwanzigste**	21.
zweiundzwanzig[1]	22	**der zweiundzwanzigste**[1]	22.
dreißig	30	**der dreißigste**	30.
vierzig	40	**der vierzigste**	40.

1. **zwo** often replaces **zwei** in speech, to distinguish it clearly from **drei**: **zwo, zwoundzwanzig** *etc*.

2. The ordinal number and the preceding definite article (and adjective if there is one) are declined e.g.:
sie ist die zehnte *she's the tenth*
bei seinem dritten Versuch *at his third attempt*

fünfzig	50	**der fünfzigste**	50.
sechzig	60	**der sechzigste**	60.
siebzig	70	**der siebzigste**	70.
achtzig	80	**der achtzigste**	80.
neunzig	90	**der neunzigste**	90.
hundert	*a hundred*	**der hundertste**	100.
einhundert	*one hundred*		
hunderteins	101	**der hunderterste**	101.
hundertzwei	102	**der hundertzweite**	102.
hunderteinundzwanzig	121	**der hunderteinundzwanzigste**	121.
zweihundert	200	**der zweihundertste**	200.
tausend	*a thousand*	**der tausendste**	1000.
eintausend	*one thousand*		
tausendeins	1001	**der tausenderste**	1001.
zweitausend	2000	**der zweitausendste**	2000.
hunderttausend	100 000	**der hunderttausendste**	100 000.
eine Million	1 000 000	**der millionste**	1 000 000.

- With large numbers, spaces or full stops are used where English uses a comma e.g.:
  1.000.000 or 1 000 000 for 1,000,000 (*a million*).

- Decimals are written with a comma instead of a full stop e.g.:
  7,5 (**sieben Komma fünf**) for 7.5 (*seven point five*).

Fractions

halb	half (a)
die Hälfte	half (the)
eine halbe Stunde	half an hour
das Drittel	third
das Viertel	quarter
zwei Drittel	two thirds
dreiviertel	three quarters
anderthalb/eineinhalb	one and a half
zweieinhalb	two and a half

Time

Wie spät ist es?	What time is it?
Wieviel Uhr ist es?	

Es ist ...	It's ...

00.00	**Mitternacht / null Uhr / vierundzwanzig Uhr / zwölf Uhr**
00.10	**zehn (Minuten) nach zwölf / null Uhr zehn**
00.15	**Viertel nach zwölf / null Uhr fünfzehn**
00.30	**halb eins / null Uhr dreißig**
00.40	**zwanzig (Minuten) vor eins / null Uhr vierzig**
00.45	**viertel vor eins / dreiviertel eins / null Uhr fünfundvierzig**
01.00	**ein Uhr**
01.10	**zehn (Minuten) nach eins / ein Uhr zehn**
01.15	**Viertel nach eins / ein Uhr fünfzehn**
01.30	**halb zwei / ein Uhr dreißig**
01.40	**zwanzig (Minuten) vor zwei / ein Uhr vierzig**
01.45	**viertel vor zwei / dreiviertel zwei / ein Uhr fünfundvierzig**
01.50	**zehn (Minuten) vor zwei / ein Uhr fünfzig**
12.00	**zwölf Uhr**
12.30	**halb eins / zwölf Uhr dreißig**
13.00	**ein Uhr / dreizehn Uhr**
16.30	**halb fünf / sechzehn Uhr dreißig**
22.00	**zehn Uhr / zweiundzwanzig Uhr / zwoundzwanzig Uhr**

morgen um halb drei at half past two tomorrow
um drei Uhr (nachmittags) at three (pm)
kurz vor zehn Uhr just before ten
gegen vier Uhr (nachmittags) towards four (in the afternoon)
erst um halb neun not until half past eight
ab neun Uhr from nine o'clock onwards
morgen früh/abend tomorrow morning/evening

The Calendar

Dates

Der wievielte ist heute?	What's the date today?
Welches Datum haben wir heute?	

Heute ist ...	It's ...
der zwanzigste März	the twentieth of March
der Zwanzigste	the twentieth

Heute haben wir ...	It's ...
den zwanzigsten März	the twentieth of March
den Zwanzigsten	the twentieth

Am wievielten findet es statt?	When does it take place?
Es findet am ersten April statt	... on the first of April
Es findet am Ersten statt	... on the first

Es findet (am) Montag, den ersten April statt
Es findet Montag, den 1. April statt
It takes place on Monday, the first of April/April 1st

Years

(im Jahre) 1994 (neunzehnhundertvierundneunzig) in 1994
Er wurde 1970 (neunzehnhundertsiebzig) geboren
He was born in 1970

Other Expressions

Im Dezember/Januar *etc* in December/January *etc*
im Winter/Sommer/Herbst/Frühling
in winter/summer/autumn/spring
Anfang September at the beginning of September
nächstes Jahr next year

Punctuation

German punctuation differs from English in the following cases:

Commas

- Decimal places are always shown by a comma (→**1**)

- Large numbers are separated off by means of a space or a full stop (→**2**)

- Subordinate clauses are always marked off from the rest of the sentence by a comma (→**3**)
  This applies to all types of subordinate clause e.g.:

  clauses with an adverbial function (→**3**)

  relative clauses (→**4**)

  clauses containing indirect speech (→**5**)

- A comma is not required between two main clauses linked by a co-ordinating conjunction (→**6**)

Exclamation Marks

- An exclamation mark is occasionally used after the name at the beginning of a letter, but this tends to be rather old-fashioned (→**7**)

- Exclamation marks are used after imperative forms unless these are not intended as commands (→**8**)

1 **3,4 (drei Komma vier)** 3.4 (three point four)

2 **20 000** *OR* **20.000 (zwanzigtausend)**
   20,000 (twenty thousand)

3 **Als er nach Hause kam, war sie schon weg**
   She had already gone when he came home
   Er bleibt gesund, obwohl er zuviel trinkt
   He stays healthy, even though he drinks too much

4 **Der Mann, mit dem sie verheiratet ist, soll sehr reich sein**
   The man she is married to is said to be very rich

5 **Er sagt, es gefällt ihm nicht**
   He says he doesn't like it

6 **Ich möchte hin aber ich darf nicht**
   I would love to go but I can't

7 **Liebe Elke!** ... Dear Elke, ...
   Sehr geehrter Herr Braun! ... Dear Mr. Braun, ...

8 **Steh auf!** Get up
   Bitte nehmen Sie doch Platz
   Do please sit down

The following index lists comprehensively both grammatical terms and key words in German and English contained in this book.

ab 72
abbreviations 106
aber 196, 214
abgewöhnen, sich 32
abhängen 44, 78
able, to be 52
ablehnen 84
about 204, 208
about, to be 42
above 210
abstract nouns 120
according to 204
accusative 108, 118
ach 226
across 210
active 34
address forms 160
adjectival nouns 148
adjectives 102
  + dative 146
  comparison 152
  declension 140
  mixed declension 142
  strong declension 130, 142
  used as nouns 98, 108, 148
  used attributively 140
  used non-attributively 140

weak declension 130, 140
adverbs 188, 224
  comparison 194
  formation 190
  of place 192
after 204, 222
against 206, 208
agent 34
ähnlich 146
all 128, 130, 186
aller 128, 186
allein 226
allerhand 144
allerlei 144
alles 130
allowed, to be 52
along 206
als 64, 222
als ob 44, 222
also 226
although 222
always 190
among 210
amüsieren, sich 78
an 72, 164, 200
anbieten 80
and 214
ander 138, 186
aneignen, sich 32
Angst 113
anhören 84
anliegen 44

ansehen 84
ansehen, sich 32
anstatt ... zu 48
anticipatory object 84
any 144
anziehen, sich 32
Apfel 112
apply for, to 32, 78
ärgern, sich 78
around 208
articles 128
  definite 118
  indefinite 124
as 222
as far as 222
as if 44, 64, 222
as soon as 222
ask for, to 78
at 208, 210
at once 190
auch 20, 226
auf 72, 164, 198, 200, 210
aufregen, sich 32
aufs 198
aus 72, 164, 202
aushalten 84
außerhalb 212
außerordentlich 156
äußerst 156, 190
auxiliary verbs, 22, 24, 220

Baby 114
baby 114
bald 194
bank account 114
be- 70
because 222
because of 212
beeilen, sich 32
before 210, 222
begegnen 24, 80
beginnen 86
begreifen 84
behind 210
bei 72, 164, 198, 200, 202
beide 128, 130, 186
beiderseits 212
beim 198
bekannt 146
bereuen 84
beschäftigen, sich 32, 78
beside 210
besonders 156, 190
besser 156
best 192
beste, der 156
bestehen 78
bestens 192
better 192
bevor 222
beweisen 80
bewerben, sich 32, 78
bis 222
bißchen 144

bitten 78
bleiben 24, 46, 86
Bonbon 114
boss 114
both 128, 186
both ... and 216
boy 115
brauchen 54
brennen 16, 86
Brille 114
bring, to 16
bringen 16, 80, 86
burn, to 16
but 214
by 34, 208
calendar 239
can 52
cardinal numbers 102, 236
care, to take c. of 78
case 76, 98, 108, 118, 124, 198
Chef 114
-chen 102
chief 114
close to 146
close, to get c. to 32
club 114
co-ordinating conjunctions 214
cold 44
comma 114, 237, 240
use of 220
comparative 152
of adverbs 194
comparison of

adjectives 152
comparison of adverbs 194
complement 108
compound nouns 106
compound tenses 6, 22, 56, 62, 220, 230
conditional 22, 28, 64
use of 58
conditional passive 40
conditional perfect 22, 28, 64
use of 60
passive 36, 40
conjunctions 214
co-ordinating 214
subordinating 220
consist of, to 78
continuous tenses 58
could 52
countries 120
da 82, 222
da- 72, 76, 164
Dach 113
daher 192
dahin 192
damit 222
dankbar 146
danken 80
dann 64, 214
dar- 72, 76, 164, 180
darauf 82

darin 82
das 84, 118, 130, 174
daß 46, 66, 84, 228
date 239
dative 36, 110, 118, 122
  plural 98, 110
  singular 110, 148
davon 72
days of the week 100
dazu 72
decimal point 114
decimals 237
declension endings 98
declension of adjectives 140, 148
definite article 118
  omission of 122
  uses of 120
dein 136
deiner 166
deinige 168
dem 118, 174
den 118, 174
denen 174
denken 16, 78, 86
denn 196, 214, 226
depend, to 44, 78
der 118, 146, 174
deren 174
derjenige 132, 186
derselbe 132, 186
des 118
dessen 174

dich 158, 170
die 118, 174
die of, to 78
dies 130
dieser 128, 134, 148, 166, 186
diminutives 102
dir 158, 170
direct object 36, 80, 108, 224
direct questions 178, 232
direct speech 230
doch 20, 196, 232, 234
donnern 42
dorthin 192
double prefixes 68, 74
doubt, expressions of 64
Drama 114
drama 114
dream of, to 78
Drittel 237
du 158, 160
durch 34, 74, 164, 200, 206
dürfen 52, 86
during 202, 212
each 122, 128, 186
each other 172
eben 58
egal 44
eher 194
ehesten 194
ein 72, 124, 148

einander 172
einbilden, sich 32
eine 124
einem 124, 158
einen 124, 158
einer 124, 184
eines 124
einfallen 42
einige 130, 144
einiger 128, 186
either ... or 218
emp- 70
emphasizers 196
emphatic reflexive pronouns 172
empor 72
endlich 190
English 150
ent- 70
entgegen 72
entlang 206
entweder ... oder 218
er 158, 162
er- 70
erinnern, sich 32, 78
erlauben, sich 32
ertragen 84
erzählen 80
es 42, 82, 158, 162
essen 86
etwas 144, 186
euch 158, 170
euer 136
euerer 166
euerige 168

eurer 166
eurige 168
even if 64
even though 64
everywhere 192
exclamation marks 240
extremely 190
fahren 86
fairly 90
fallen 88
familiar forms 160
familiar to 146
fangen 88
fehlen 80
feminine 98
  nouns 104
fest 72
few 138, 144
few, a f. 144
fewer 144
fight for, to 78
finally 190
fine, to be 42
firm 114
Firma 114
for 204, 206, 208, 214
foreign nouns 100, 102
formal address form 160
fractions 102, 237
fragen 42
Frau 119
freeze, to 42
frei 72

fremd 146
freuen 42
freuen, sich 32, 78
frieren 42
from 202, 204
für 164, 200, 206
furchtbar 156
future tense 22, 28
  use of 58
future passive subjunctive 40
future perfect 22, 28
  use of 58
  passive 36, 40
future subjunctive 22, 28
ganz 130
ge- 50, 70, 72, 74
geben 80, 88
gefallen 42, 80
gegen 206
gegenüber 202
gehen 42, 44, 46, 88
gehen um 42
gehören 80
gelingen 24, 42, 80, 88
gender 98, 124
  of nouns 100
Genie 104
genitive 110, 118, 120
  singular 98, 110,

116, 142
genitive personal pronouns 162
geographical names 120
gerade 58
German 150
gern 194
geschehen 42, 88
gewöhnen, sich 78
gibt, es 82
gießen 42
give up, to 32
glad, to be 42
glasses 114
gleich 146
gleichen 80
gönnen 80, 84
goodbye, to say g. to 78
gratulieren 80
gut 42, 44, 156
haben 22, 24, 26, 28, 30, 88, 146
halb 237
half 237
Hälfte 237
halten 88
handeln, sich h. um 42
happen, to 42, 44
have to, to 54
he 158
head 114
heißen 46
Held 115

helfen 80
her 72, 136, 158, 192
herab 72
heran 72
herauf 72, 164
heraus 72, 164
herausstellen, sich 44
herbei 72
here 192
herein 72, 164
hero 115
Herr 116
hers 166
herself 170
herüber 72
herum 72
herunter 72
hervor 72
heute 190, 238
hierher 72
him 158
himself 170
hin 72
hinab 72
hinauf 72, 164
hinaus 72, 164
hindurch 72
hinein 72, 164
hinsetzen, sich 32
hinsichtlich 212
hinter 74, 200, 210
hinüber 72
hinunter 72
his 136, 166
hoch 146, 156

höchst 154
höchste, der 156
höher 156
Hose 114
hot 44
Hotel 114
hotel 114
however 214
hurry, to 32
I 158
ich 158
if 62
if only 64
ihm 158
ihn 158
ihnen 158
Ihnen 158
ihr 136, 158, 160
Ihr 136
ihrer 166
Ihrer 166
ihrige 168
Ihrige 168
imagine, to 32
immer 190, 194
imperative 18, 30, 48, 240
    alternatives to 20
    word order 230
imperfect tense 6, 8, 12, 14, 16
    use of 60
imperfect passive 38
    subjunctive 38
imperfect subjunctive 6, 12,

16, 62
impersonal verbs 42
imponieren 80
important 44
in 164, 200, 210
in front of 210
in spite of 212
inclined, to be i. to 78
indefinite adjectives 138
indefinite article 124
indefinite pronouns 182
indem 222
indicative 64
indicative tenses 62
indirect object 36, 80, 110, 224
indirect questions 178, 232
indirect speech 66, 240
    word order 230
infinitive 8, 20, 28, 46, 72, 84
    + modal verbs 48
    after adjectives 46
    after verbs 46
    passive 40
    perfect active 47
    perfect passive 40, 47
    phrases 48, 230
    present active 47
    present passive 47

used as noun 48, 102
infolge 212
innerhalb 212
inseparable prefixes 70
inseparable verbs 50, 68
inside 212
instead of 212
interessieren 44
interessieren, sich 32, 78
interested, to be 32, 44, 78
interrogative adjectives 232
interrogative adverbs 232
interrogative pronouns 178, 232
interrogative words 232
into 210
intransitive verbs 24, 42
inversion 30, 214, 218
inwiefern 222
irgendein 136, 148
irgendwelcher 128
irren, sich 32
isn't it? 232
Israeli 114
ist, es 82
it 158

its 136, 166
itself 170
ja 196, 226, 234
Jahr 238
je ... desto 194
je ... um so 194
jeder 128, 135, 186
jemand 182
jener 128, 134, 186
jenseits 212
Junge 115, 148
kalt 44
kämpfen 78
kaufen 80
kein 126, 148, 234
keine 126
keinem 126
keinen 126
keiner 126, 184
keinerlei 144
keines 126
kennen 16, 90
Kind 119
klingeln 44
klopfen 44
Klub 114
knock, to 44
know, to 16
Komma 114
kommen 90
  es kommt darauf an 44
können 52, 90, 220
Konto 114
kümmern, sich 78
lassen 46, 90

lassen, sich 34
laufen 90
laugh at, to 78
läuten 44
lauter 44
leicht 146
leid tun 44
leiden 78
leider 190
leihen 80
-lein 102
leisten, sich 32
lesen 90
less 144
letters 240
leugnen 84
lieber 194
liebsten 193
like 222
like, to 42, 52
little 128
little, a l. 138, 144, 186
lohnen, sich 44
long for, to 78
look around, to 32
look forward to, to 32, 78
los 72
machen, es macht nichts 44
main clauses 220
mal 20, 196
man 34, 36, 158, 162
manch 144
mancher 128, 186

mancherlei 144
Mann 119
many 138, 144
masculine nouns 98
matter, to 44
may 52
me 158
meals, names of
 120
measurement,
 nouns of 116
mehr 144, 156, 186
mehrere 138, 186
mehrerlei 144
mein 136
meiner 166
meinige 168
meiste, der 156
meistens 192
melden, sich 32
member 104
mich 158, 170
mine 166
mir 158, 170
miß- 70
mißtrauen 80
mit 72, 164, 202,
 204
Mitglied 104
mitteilen 80
mixed declension of
 adjectives 142
mixed verbs 6, 16,
 24, 68
modal verbs 46, 52,
 220

past participle 56
mögen 52, 90, 220
möglich 44
montags 214
months 100, 122
more 144, 186
morgen 190, 238
morgens 190
Mr 116
much 144
müssen 52, 54, 90
must 52, 54
my 136
myself 170
nach 72, 122, 164,
 202, 204
nachdem 222
nachdenken 78
nachgehen 80
nachmittags 238
nächste, der 156
nah 146, 156
näher 156
nähern, sich 32
name, to 16
nationality 150
near 202
neben 164, 210
necessary 44
negatives 234
nehmen 90
neigen 78
nein 226
neither ... nor 216
nennen 16, 90
neuter 98

never 234
nicht 232, 234
nicht nur ...
 sondern auch 218
nicht wahr 232
nichts 186
nie 234
nieder 72
niemand 182
Niveau 114
no one 182
nobody 182
nominative 108,
 118
nominative plural
 108
nominative singular
 98, 108
none 186
not 234
not only ... but also
 218
nothing 186
nötig 44, 84
nouns 98
 compound 106
 declension 98, 112
 feminine 104
 gender 100
 number 6, 98
nun 226
nur 20, 226
ob 228
oben 190
objects 224
 direct 108

indirect 110
obwohl 222
occur, to 42
oder 214, 226
ohne 206, 208
ohne ... zu 48
on 210
one 158
  pronoun 34, 162
Onkel 112
opposite 202
or 214
ordinal numbers 236
orphan 104
other 138, 186
ought 54
our 136
ours 166
ourselves 170
out of 202
outside 212
over 210
paar 144, 186
park 114
Park 114
participles 102, 148
  as adjectives 146
  past 50
  present 50
partly 218
parts of the body 122
passieren 44
passive 34, 162
passive infinitive 40
passive tenses 38

past participles 12, 16, 24, 26, 38, 50, 70, 72
peinlich 146
per 122
perception, verbs of 46
perfect tense 22, 26
  use of 60
perfect infinitive 28, 47
  passive 47
perfect passive subjunctive 38
perfect passive infinitive 40
perfect subjunctive 22, 26
person, 6, 104
Person 104
personal names 116
personal pronouns 158
pity, it's a p. 44
place names 150
plan, to 32
pleased, to be p. about 78
pluperfect tense 22, 26
  use of 60
pluperfect passive 38
  subjunctive 40
pluperfect subjunctive 22, 26, 36, 60, 64

plural 98
  formation 112
polite form 160, 170
possessive adjectives 122, 136
possessive pronouns 166
  alternative forms 168
possible 42, 44
pour, to 42
prefixes 68
  double 74
  inseparable 70
  separable 72
  variable 74
prepositions 108, 198
  + accusative 108, 206
  + dative or accusative 210
  + dative 110, 202
  + genitive 110, 212
  contracted forms 200
present tense, 6, 8, 12, 14
  use of 58
present infinitive 47
  passive 47
present participle 50
present passive subjunctive 38

present subjunctive 6, 12
price, expressions of 122
principle 114
Prinzip 114
pronoun objects 226
pronouns 128
  after prepositions 164
  indefinite 182
  interrogative 178
  personal 164
  possessive 166
  reflexive 170
  relative 174
proper names 116, 120
punctuation 240
quantity, nouns of 116
quarter 237
question, to be a q. of 42
questions 232
  direct 178
  indirect 178
rain, to 44
rasieren, sich 32
reflexive pronouns 30, 48, 122, 170, 224, 228
reflexive verbs 18, 30, 170
regnen 44
regular verbs 8

relative clauses 174, 176, 240
relative pronouns 174, 228
rely on, to 78
remember, to 32, 78
rennen 16, 92
report, to 32
reported speech 62, 66
restaurant 104, 114
Restaurant 104, 114
richtig 156
riechen 78
ring, to 44
Risiko 114
risk 114
run, to 16
sämtliche 128, 186
sämtlicher 130
schade 44
schaden 80
scheinen 44
schenken 80
Schere 114
schicken 80
Schicksal 113
schlafen 92
schlagen 92
schlecht 42, 44
schließen 92
schmecken 78, 80
schmeicheln 80
schneien 44
schon 196

schreiben 80
schulden 80
Schweiz 150
scissors 114
seasons 100, 120
seem, to 44
sehen 94
sehnen, sich 78
sehr 156
sein 136
sein (vb) 20, 22, 24, 26, 28, 30, 38, 40, 46, 94, 108, 146
seiner 166
seinige 168
seit 58, 60, 122, 202, 204
seitdem 58, 60, 222
selber 172
selbst 172
selbst wenn 64
send, to 16
senden 16, 94
separable prefixes 72
separable verbs, 18, 48, 50, 68
setzen, sich 32
several 138, 144, 186
shall have done 58
shave, to 32
she 158
should 52, 54
sich 30, 170
sie 158, 162
Sie 158, 160

similar to 146
simple tenses 6, 56, 62
since 204, 222
sind, es 82
singular 98
sit down, to 32
smell of, to 78
smile, to 78
snow, to 44
so daß 222
so that 222
sobald 222
sofort 190
sogar 226
solch 144
solcher 128, 130, 186
sollen 52, 54, 64, 94
some 128, 136, 144, 186
someone 182
something 186
somewhere 192
sondern 214, 226, 234
soon 194
sooner 194
soonest 194
sorry, to be 44
soweit 222
sowohl ... als 216
spät 238
spelling of adjectives 146
sprechen 94

standard 114
statt 212
stem, 6, 8
sterben 78
stimmen 44
stoßen 94
Streik 114
strike 114
strong declension of adjectives 130, 142
strong verbs 6, 12, 18, 24, 50, 68
vowel changes 14
Stuhl 113
subject 6, 108, 224
subjunctive 38, 40, 60
in indirect speech 66
uses of 62
subordinate clauses 220, 228, 240
subordinating conjunctions 220, 228
succeed, to 42
such 128, 144, 186
suffer from, to 78
superlative 154, 156
of adverbs 194
supposed to, to be 54
sweet 114
talk about, to 78
taste of, to 78
teilnehmen 78
teils 218
tenses 6

compound 22
simple 6
than 222
that 66, 128, 186
the 118
their 136
theirs 166
them 158
Thema 114
themselves 170
there 192
there are 82
there is 82
they 158
impersonal use 34
think about, to 78
think, to 16
third 237
this 128, 186
through 206
thunder, to 42
time 238
to 202, 204, 206, 210
today 190
tomorrow 190, 238
topic 114
towards 202, 206
tragen 96
trauen 80
trauen, sich 32
träumen 78
tremble, to 78
trinken 96
trotz 212
trotzdem 214
trotzen 80
trousers 114

trust oneself, to 32
tun 96
turn, to 16
über 74, 164, 200, 210
Uhr 238
um 74, 200, 206, 208
um ... zu 48
umsehen, sich 32
unbekannt 146
und 214, 226
under 210
uns 158, 170
unser 136
unserer 166
unserige 168
unsrer 166
unsrige 168
unten 190
unter 74, 164, 200, 210
unterhalten, sich 78
unternehmen 84
until 222
us 158
variable prefixes 68, 74
various 144
ver- 70
verabschieden, sich 78
verb endings 8
verbieten 84
verbs 6
  + dative 80, 110

+ prepositions 76
inseparable 50, 68
mixed 6, 16
reflexive 170
regular 8
separable 50, 68, 230
strong 6, 12, 50
weak 6, 8, 50
with prefixes 68
vergeben 84
verkaufen 80
verlassen, sich 78
verschweigen 84
verstehen 84
verstehen, sich 78
verzeihen 84
viel 138, 144, 156
vielerlei 144
Viertel 237
voll 74
von 34, 200, 202, 204
vor 72, 122, 200, 210
vorangehen 80
vorbei 72
vorkommen 44
vornehmen, sich 32
vorstellen, sich 32
vorüber 72
Wache 104
wagen 84
während 212, 222

Waise 104
wait for, to 78
wann 222
want, to 32, 54
warm 44
warten 78
was 176, 178, 180
was für 144, 180
we 158
weak declension of adjectives 130, 140
weak masculine nouns 108, 115
weak verbs 6, 8, 18, 24, 50, 68
special features 10
weder ... noch 216
weg 72
wegen 162, 212
weh tun 80
Weib 104
weil 222
welch 144
welche 176
welchem 176
welchen 176
welcher 128, 135, 176, 180, 186
welcherlei 144
welches 176
well 192
wem 178
wen 178
wenden 16, 96
wenig 138, 144, 186
weniger 144

wenigstens 192
wenn 62, 64, 222, 228
wenn ... nur 64
wer 176, 178
werden 22, 24, 28, 34, 38, 40, 96, 108
werfen 96
wessen 178
what 176
what a 144
when 222
whenever 222
where 192, 222
whereupon 222
which 128
while 222
who 176
wichtig 44
wider 74, 206, 208
widersprechen 80
widerstehen 80
wie 46, 76, 222
wieder 74
wievielerlei 144
wife 104
will have done 58

willen 162
willing, to be 54
wir 158
wissen 16, 96
with 204
within 212
without 208
wo 222
wo- 174, 180
woher 180, 192
wohin 180, 192, 222
wollen 52, 54, 64, 96
woman 104
wonder, to 42
wor- 174, 180
worauf 222
word order 80, 214
  main clauses 224
  subordinate
    clauses 228
  with modal verbs
    56
  with separable
    verbs 72
worden 38, 40

worin 222
wrong, to be 32
wünschen, sich 32
years 238
yes 232
you 158
your 136
yours 166
yourself 170
yourselves 170
zeigen 80
zer- 70
ziemlich 190
zittern 78
zu 46, 48, 72, 84, 198, 200, 202, 204
zur 198
zurecht 72
zurück 72
zusammen 72
zutrauen 84
Zweck 44
zwei 144
zweierlei 144
zwischen 164, 210
zwo 236